A Death in the Family

The death of someone close is one of the hardest of
life's experiences. Family and friends are faced with
a bewildering series of decisions and arrangements,
often for the first time. This book is designed to help
with all these practical matters, explaining them and
making them as easy as possible.

But the emotional and spiritual side is even more
important than the practical questions. Jean
Richardson writes out of her own experience as a
widow left to bring up a family. She also draws on the
experience of others as she guides the reader through
the various stages of grief. Her book, written from the
perspective of Christian belief, is thoughtful and
reassuring, full of practical help and real hope for the
future.

Jean Richardson's husband died suddenly and
unexpectedly in 1965. Her three sons were then
aged eight, thirteen and sixteen. Not wanting to take
a full-time job while they were still at school, she
became a freelance writer. She has written and
spoken widely on the subjects of bereavement and
one-parent families, and has become well-known as
a regular broadcaster in 'Prayer for the Day',
'Woman's Hour' an

D1422353

A Death in the Family

Jean Richardson

A LION PAPERBACK
Oxford · Batavia · Sydney

Text copyright 1979 and 1993 Jean Richardson
Second edition © 1993 Lion Publishing

The author asserts the moral right
to be identified as the author of this work

Published by
Lion Publishing plc
Sandy Lane West, Oxford, England
ISBN 0 7459 2387 9
Albatross Books Pty Ltd
PO Box 320, Sutherland, NSW 2232, Australia
ISBN 0 7324 0628 5

First edition 1979
Second edition 1993

All rights reserved

Acknowledgments
The following books have been helpful in the preparation of this
book:
C. Murray Parkes, *Bereavement*, Pelican
Sarah Morris, *Grief and how to live with it*, Allen & Unwin
Katie Wiebe, *Alone*, Marshall, Morgan & Scott
C.S. Lewis, *A Grief Observed*, Faber & Faber
Anne Hopkinson, *Families Without Fathers*, Mothers' Union.
Some additional information and text by Rosemary A. Crewe have
been incorporated.

Printed and bound in Great Britain
by Cox & Wyman Ltd, Reading

Contents

Introduction

Death has suddenly become personal; it has hit where it hurts most, and you find you have to live the rest of your life without someone you love or have loved.

This book has been written to help with the practical questions, emotional problems and spiritual matters: how to arrange a funeral, deal with a will, understand your irritability, let a room, find a job, and everything in between. There are also sections on grief and mourning to help you understand why you feel as you do, and what you can do to help yourself and those around you through this difficult time.

Security

Bereavement snatches away our most basic human security. Our world crumbles, and we wonder, desperately, how we can go on. The way in which we handle a crisis such as this depends much on our attitudes and beliefs. Personally, as a Christian, I could not have survived being widowed without the presence and strength of God, the prayers of fellow Christians and the support of friends.

Make or break

An experience of such depth and magnitude as the death of a member of our family can either make or break us; it can destroy us, or it can mark a growing-point which leads to a new beginning. Death is part of life and it cannot be avoided; some time or other in life everyone comes face to face with it. It is often unexpected, always unwelcome and always causes pain.

With the pain come all sorts of other symptoms, and they usually follow a pattern—almost like an illness. As with an illness, with care and help, we recover, but while the illness lasts we see no end to it. Such is bereavement.

No two people come through it the same. Since I lost my husband, six other close members of my family have also died, including a dearly loved brother. And so I have come to understand a little more clearly the meaning of grief and how little prepared most of us are to cope with it.

I was already a Christian before my husband's death and the family had close connections with our local parish church. Bereavement put our faith to many tests, but it survived them all. Our shared experience has drawn us all closer to each other, although we are all now separated, physically.

In this book, I have drawn heavily on personal experience of the problems and difficulties—as well as some of the unexpected compensations—of widowhood, bringing up a family single-handed and the effects of bereavement many years on.

1
Preparing for Bereavement

Who would prepare for bereavement? Death is the forbidden topic of our age: it's hard enough to talk about even when it strikes someone you know, so why drag it up when there is no apparent need? Surely, preparing for bereavement is simply morbid.

Yet my experience has taught me otherwise. I shall always be glad that my husband and I once discussed the inevitable fact that one of us would die before the other. Medical evidence shows that being prepared does help the bereaved person, and lessens the confusion which follows any death. Apart from the advantage of knowing where to turn for help, there will be the comfort of knowing what you had decided together.

MAKING A WILL

Everyone should make a will, even if there seems little of value to leave. Otherwise, when a person dies, the family simply won't know what they wanted done with their belongings, and there could be needless legal problems.

Without a will, the main problem could be that, as all assets are frozen at death, family members may not be able to get hold of any money until all legal formalities have been completed. This can be devastating to a surviving partner or other dependants.

An additional way to avoid the problem is to ensure that somewhere there is a sum of money which can tide the bereaved over for a short while. Even a little in a joint bank or building society account can be a great help.

To avoid legal pitfalls, it is best for a solicitor to draw up the will. The cost of this varies, so ask about charges in advance. Then, in the UK, you simply make an appointment and take with you the following:

O the names of two people who have agreed to act as executors

O the names of people you want to inherit your property, whether specific items or a proportion.

The solicitor prepares the will, which you then read in draft form. Once you have approved its contents a final copy is prepared which you sign in the presence of two witnesses. Witnesses must be people who do not benefit under the will, and if you go to the solicitor's office to approve the final copy they will usually be the solicitor and another member of the office staff. It is best to let the solicitor keep the will safe, and for you to keep a copy at home with the solicitor's address.

Remember that getting married may cancel any previous will. In the UK, after a divorce, a former spouse gets nothing unless the will clearly states otherwise. This ruling varies from country to country.

Executors

The executors make sure that what the will asks for actually happens. They are responsible for paying, from the estate, all the deceased's debts, taxes, bills, and the cost of the funeral. They will then distribute the moneys, possessions, property and general effects according to the instructions in the will. Executors may be beneficiaries. Ex-spouses cannot act as executors.

Children

Remember to make provision for any children, both financially and for their upbringing. There is a possibility, however small, that the parents may both be killed, and so the will should say who is to be responsible for the children. The people you choose as guardians need to agree, of course.

When considering who they should be, the interest of

the children must come first. It is wise to bear in mind that the people you would trust to look after young children may not necessarily be the same people you would want to see them through their teens, so this section of the will, particularly, needs to be kept up to date.

Some children worry about the possibility of their parents dying; if they ask 'What will happen to us if you both die?' they can be reassured to know that someone, whom they know and trust, will look after them.

SORTING OUT YOUR AFFAIRS

Your house

It is important to make sure that a death in the family won't leave you or your loved ones with a housing crisis.

○ If you are buying your house as a joint venture, make sure that your life insurance is linked to the mortgage—it is essential to know that you will still have a roof over your head if one of the people contributing to the mortgage dies.

○ If the house is already your own, discuss whether you could still afford to live there if one person were to die.

○ If you rent your home, is the lease in one person's name only? If so, then the others may be given notice to leave when that person dies.

○ If the house is rented from the local council (as can happen in the UK), you should find out how things operate in your area: phone them and ask. Some will transfer a tenancy, but some will ask you to find somewhere else to live—although they are obliged to rehouse an existing tenant.

Money and documents

Having made your will, it is a good idea to keep a list of all the documents you will need following a death with a note of where to find them.

Do you know where they are?

Documents such as

◇ wills, especially if they contain instructions for the funeral

◇ bank/building society pass books and account numbers

◇ birth/marriage certificates

◇ savings books

◇ stocks and shares certificates

◇ rent book

◇ driving licence

◇ passport

◇ season tickets

◇ deeds of house

◇ insurance policies

◇ motor insurance certificate

◇ cheque/credit cards

◇ TV licence (if applicable)

◇ NHS number

◇ car log book/break-down service details

Documents relating to

◇ bank loans

◇ pensions

◇ trade union/professional body membership number

◇ mortgage/hire purchase repayments

◇ receipts of paid bills

Addresses of

◇ doctor

◇ solicitor

◇ executors

In times of stress, we do not think clearly and memories are faulty, so make sure you know where all the important documents which may have to be produced are kept. You don't need to understand everything involved, but to have a grasp of the basics will make all the difference.

COPING WITH SERIOUS ILLNESS

Sometimes death strikes without warning, but more often there is a period of illness first. Although this is a harrowing time, it can be used in some degree to prepare the family for bereavement if it should come.

Life has changed; it has narrowed to visits to the hospital, long hours at the bedside or the months and years of a degenerative disease. There is a feeling of panic and of resentment. Severe illness is an emotional drain for everyone, and it helps to recognize this and to adjust to living from one day to the next.

Learn to shorten your time scale so that your new, circumscribed life is divided into manageable chunks. Don't look *too* far ahead, otherwise wild imaginings will go out of control and you will be overwhelmed. Try not to repress your feelings—it is natural from time to time to feel angry. A friend of mine waited until she was alone in the house and then went from room to room deliberately slamming all the doors. She said this released the pent up resentment which had been eating at her all that day.

For Christians, it should be easier to discuss openly what is happening. If the sick person is still mentally aware, it can be a source of comfort to face the future together and to discuss plans for the one left and for the family, drawing on the promises of God that life goes on after death and that his loving protection will embrace those left behind.

Handling the situation

However feeble the patient may be, treat them normally, not like a baby. Try to understand their needs—if they want to talk, let them; if they want you to talk, then do so calmly and normally. One friend of mine, Martin, said,'My own world has become so small now, that I just want to hear about trivial day-to-day things; I can't cope with anything bigger.'

Try to organize your day so as to have a time for yourself, however short, to regain a sense of proportion. Don't feel guilty about wanting to 'get away'—you will be all the more use when you return. Never impose unrealistically high standards on yourself—you won't be able to keep them up and everyone, not only the patient, will suffer. Above all, never refuse offers of help.

Elizabeth was one of those people who would drop

everything to go to someone in trouble. She shopped, washed, ironed and cooked for them all. But, like many helpers, she was always reluctant to receive help in return. When her husband became incurably ill, she cut herself off, devoted all her time and energies to looking after him twenty-four hours a day and made it clear that she could 'manage' perfectly well on her own. Sadly, her friends had to accept her rejection of them and, when she was eventually alone, only a few felt able to pick up the threads of friendship again.

Find out about organizations that may be able to offer specific advice. These days, there are nearly as many support groups as there are illnesses, diseases and various bereavement problems. Your doctor may be able to suggest which one is most relevant to you. Alternatively, your local library will have a list of them.

RELATIONSHIPS

Another way to prepare for bereavement is to lead a full and friendly life. It is never good for a family to be so self-sufficient and dependent on each other that they exclude other people. Old friendships should be kept up and new ones formed all the way through life. As you get older, you will get great enjoyment from building friendships with people younger than yourself, and they will benefit from knowing you. A special bonus is that, as members of your own generation become fewer, you will not be left with only old or ageing people with whom to mix. The loneliness of bereavement, if it strikes, will be lessened by the care and concern of all sorts of people.

Children who are brought up in a home where people are always coming and going learn to be outgoing and friendly and benefit from different outlooks and relationships. They, too, should be encouraged to make new friends, especially if they have no siblings, so that they will be able to draw on a broad spectrum of support in times of stress or trouble and will have a variety of friends to turn to. One ten year old told his granny, after his mother had died,

'I don't know who I'll play with tomorrow—I shall have to see how I'm feeling.'

Sharing the work

When people live together as a family or household, it's only natural that they should share out the work and benefit from each other's special talents for different types of jobs. However, it's also good not to become so dependent on each other that daily routines cease to function if one member of the household dies. Everyone should have some idea of how to get the laundry done, what to do when electrical appliances break down, how to put a meal together, and so on. The grown-ups should all have some grasp of the basic family finances and be able to deal with a budget, however simple. Being able to drive the family car can be very important.

Teach the children any jobs within their scope. Boys and girls alike will one day need to know how to fend for themselves—cooking, cleaning, repairing things and so on—and teaching them young helps build their self-esteem. These skills will be especially useful, if the family has to deal with the loss of a loved one, in keeping the household running on an even keel.

Other work interests

Maintaining interests outside work can be vital. People at any stage of their lives benefit from knowing that they are valued outside the family as well as within it. If a family member dies, those remaining still have some structure and everyday purpose to their lives. In many cases, the ability to earn enough money to support the remaining family is essential, and the period of mourning is testing enough without the worry of having to learn the ways of the working world from scratch.

2
The First Few Days

When someone we love dies, particularly someone on whom we have depended, one of our strongest emotions is likely to be sheer panic. We feel helpless. We don't know what to do. Dimly, we are aware that 'arrangements' will have to be made but we don't know what they are or how to go about them.

The first step is to call the doctor. 'What must I do?' I asked my doctor when he told me my husband was dead. 'Nothing at all for an hour or two,' he said, 'I'll send people to help you.' Later that morning, the undertaker and the rector of our church came and guided me through the decisions and arrangements which had to be made.

WHAT TO DO FIRST

First of all, it is necessary to have the death certificate. This will be issued by a hospital doctor or your GP. If the body is to be cremated, the certificate will need the signatures of two doctors—this is purely a formality and does not mean there was anything suspicious about the death itself.

Registering the death

Once the certificate has been issued, the death must be registered at the local office of the Registrar of Births, Marriages and Deaths as soon as possible (some countries have a specific time limit). This is usually done by the next of kin, but a relative, executor or friend can go to the Register Office and supply any details which may be necessary.

The Registrar will need details of the dead person. You will need to take the following with you:

○ the medical certificate stating the cause of death

○ if applicable in the UK, the pink form issued by a coroner.

The Registrar will also need to know these details:

○ the date and place of death

○ the deceased's name, address, occupation, and date and place of birth. Whether they were receiving a pension or allowance from public funds and, if the deceased was married, the date of birth of the surviving spouse.

The Registrar will then give you two documents:

○ a certificate of burial or cremation

○ a certificate of Registration of Death and leaflets about benefits and so on. It is a good idea to ask for a few extra copies of this form to use when you claim allowances and insurance payments.

Once you have registered the death, you can claim the various benefits to which you are entitled. Brief details are given here, but leaflets and advice are readily available. In the UK, for example, the Department of Social Security booklet *What to do after a death* is most helpful.

Things to send back

◇ any order book issued by the Department of Social Security (in the UK). Keep a record of the numbers

◇ membership cards of clubs/associations (claim any refund due)

◇ season ticket (claim any refund due)

◇ library books and tickets

◇ any National Insurance papers

◇ any health equipment on loan (wheelchairs, hearing aids, artificial limbs and so on)

Financial help for couples

Widows and widowers are entitled to a range of benefits.
The details are reviewed and altered periodically, and you
will need up-to-date advice on what you can obtain. Your
doctor can refer you to a social worker who can give you
this advice. This summary outlines the Department of Social
Security provisions that apply in the UK.

- **Widow's payment** A tax free lump sum paid at once,
  depending on the husband's National Insurance contributions, if you were under 65 when widowed or if your
  husband was not getting a retirement pension when he
  died

- **Widow's pension**

- **Help for widowers** One-parent benefit is also paid to
  fathers. You may be able to claim Income support, Family
  Credit, Council Tax benefit and help with NHS costs. You
  may be able to draw benefits based on your wife's National Insurance contributions or you may be entitled to
  an invalidity benefit.

You may have access to a telephone enquiry service: for
example, in England, Scotland and Wales there is the Freeline
Social Security—on 0800 666 555—which gives advice on all
Social Security and National Insurance matters.

Announcing the death

The undertaker will take on all responsibility for the funeral,
the cost of which will come out of the estate. This person
can arrange for any announcements to be inserted in local
or national newspapers and, if necessary, will help with the
wording of these. If the arrangement is for a private funeral,
only those personally asked to attend should do so. The
notice in the papers should make it clear if there are to be
no flowers or letters, and this request should also be observed: friends can always send some flowers or a plant to
the bereaved after a few days. A usual alternative is for
donations to be asked for a charity or organization in which

the deceased was particularly interested.

I am always sorry when I read in such announcements the words 'No letters'. Just at first, letters can be a burden rather than a comfort, but even those who feel they can't face them at the time often regret their decision later on. They can always be put on one side—or answered by another member of the family—and can be an unexpected source of pride and comfort after the worst of the grief has subsided.

Bereaved children will almost certainly want to know, when they are older, what friends, colleagues and relatives wrote about their dead parent or grandparent, and people outside the family usually welcome this opportunity to express their sympathy and sense of loss.

THE FUNERAL

The undertaker will need to know where the service is to take place and whether the dead person is to be buried or cremated. The undertaker will then consult the minister and/or the crematorium and suggest the day and time when the funeral can take place. They will want to know how many cars will be needed, if there are to be flowers, whether you want to follow the hearse from the house or meet it at the door of the church or crematorium. You will be asked to choose the coffin, from photographs, and you will also need to arrange for family flowers, choosing from pictures at a local florist.

Even if there is to be no church service, the undertaker will normally notify the local minister so that they can visit the bereaved family before the funeral and also a few weeks later, when the mourners may be feeling the full force of what has happened.

Costs

Funeral costs vary greatly, according to how elaborate the funeral is and where it takes place. The funeral director always pays fees on behalf of the clients and the bill covers most aspects of the funeral, such as the church service (if

Burial

◇ gravestone is a permanent memorial

◇ symbolizes being laid to rest

◇ follows biblical tradition

BUT

◇ burial is very costly

◇ grave needs tending

Cremation

◇ can be cheaper than burial

◇ symbolizes purifying release

◇ ecologically sound—saves land for the living

◇ no grave to look after

BUT

◇ some dislike the idea of being burned

◇ often no visible memorial

there is a charge), burial or cremation, hire of hearse and car, notification cards and so on. Check exactly what is covered when you ask for an estimate of funeral costs. Find out if the deceased had contributed to any special fund—an insurance policy/charity/pension scheme—that might help pay. You may also get help if you are already claiming benefits paid to people on lower incomes.

The undertakers will give you a written estimate and advice on details. They will expect to wait long enough for payment to allow for probate and the release of funds in most cases. Probate is the legal name for transferring all the dead person's property to the executors, so that they can then distribute it on the dead person's behalf.

The church service

The actual form of the service will depend on the denomination of the church where the funeral takes place. Traditionally, the minister meets the procession at the door and the coffin is carried in, followed by the mourners, who sit together in the front pews. In some places, it is now the custom for the coffin to be brought to the church a little before the service and for the mourners to take their places as they arrive, rather than to follow the coffin in procession. You may be asked which arrangement you would prefer. In either case the mourners follow the coffin out of the church at the end of the service before the rest of the congregation leaves.

The undertaker will already have asked if all the mourners are to go on to the burial ground or the crematorium or whether only the immediate family intend to do so. They will also have arranged for cars to take the mourners to the final ceremony and to the house where they will meet when it is all over.

Usually, a member of the clergy will have called on the bereaved family to explain the service or answer any questions. The service will normally follow the church's or chapel's own tradition. Most mourners and their supporters find the words of the service to be a great comfort and source of strength. When emotions are ragged and concentration difficult, the formal, dignified sentences express our deepest feelings and hopes.

An elderly widower with no church experience said after his wife's funeral, 'I'm going to ask that clergyman where I can read those words for myself—they said all the things I didn't even know I wanted to say.'

Some people, especially if they have a Christian background, like to choose readings and prayers. These are sometimes read by a member of the family or a close friend.

During the service, a short address may be given recalling the life and work of the dead person, although this is sometimes felt to add to the strain for the mourners. Even if this is so, that pain will often afterwards be seen as part of the letting go and the goodbye. Sometimes, especially if the dead person had been widely known, a memorial service is arranged on a later date to enable more distant friends and colleagues to pay their respects.

Music

Most church services include music. Often, a hymn which was a favourite of the dead person is sung, but, if you are not sure which to choose, the clergy will be able to suggest one or two. Funeral hymns need not always be slow and sad—the Christian hope is that there is new life after death and this positive approach can be reflected in hymns which are brighter than are often considered suitable for this occasion. For example, you might consider one of these:

○ Now thank we all our God

○ The day thou gavest, Lord, is ended

○ Who would true valour see

○ For all the saints who from their labours rest

○ Through all the changing scenes of life

There will generally be an organist to provide any music you may choose but it is not usual for the choir to attend unless specially asked for, except sometimes when the dead person was a prominent member of the church or community.

The crematorium service

This is a shortened form of the church service and can include music and hymns if desired. It can be conducted either by your local minister or by the chaplain attached to the crematorium. The coffin usually remains visible while the words of committal are said, then curtains are drawn across.

Any flowers or wreaths will have been placed in a small area outside the chapel where the mourners can see them after the service and read the cards; the flowers will remain there for a few days.

A service in church may be followed by a brief committal at the crematorium before cremation.

Disposal of the body

If the funeral service in church is to be followed by burial, the mourners will be taken to the burial ground for the final, very short, committal ceremony at the grave. Then the bearers lower the coffin into the grave on slings while the words of comfort and committal are said. From there, the mourners will return to the house or go their own way, according to the arrangements they have made.

Many cemeteries and churchyards now allow only a headstone (with suitable words) to be erected, in order to allow grass to be mown and the whole area kept tidy and well tended. These can be put in place after about two months when the ground has settled.

If the body was cremated, the urn containing the ashes can be buried in the area of the cemetery reserved for this. This can be done as soon as the simple memorial plaque is ready, and the short committal follows a similar pattern to the burial of a body. Where permitted, the practice of planting a rose tree alongside the plaque makes these quiet places in the churchyard or burial ground beautiful and hopeful to visit later.

Alternatively, you can arrange for the ashes to be scattered. This normally takes place in the crematorium Garden of Remembrance from one to fourteen days after the cremation. You can choose to be present if you wish.

Significance of the funeral

Every bereaved person dreads this ordeal, but, whatever form this final ceremony takes, from a psychological point of view it is most important. Even quite young children should be included in this public act of mourning.

The funeral helps to impress the fact that death *has* taken place and the need to come to terms with what has happened. Much comfort is drawn from the gathering together of family, friends and neighbours. It brings home the reality of the situation when the mind is still numb enough to be protected from all the implications. The funeral marks the end of a brief period where all seems unreal and is an essential part of mourning. (See the chapter *Mourning*.)

Coping with immediate grief

An understanding doctor will, if asked, give you something to help you through the day but it is unwise to expect any drug to be anything more than a temporary solution. After the death of her husband, a widow in public life was quoted as saying, 'Widows should be allowed to experience the grief of losing their husbands and widowers their wives without being treated with sleeping-pills and tranquillizers.' She felt sure that it is better for anyone who mourns to express grief while everyone around is being kind and helpful.

I myself feel it is better to live through a time of misery and sadness with a relatively clear head and as much dignity as one can muster, trying to realize that some aspects of life *are* tragic and have to be accepted. Most people would recover their balance and composure more quickly if doctors and well-meaning relatives would allow them to be thoroughly miserable for a time. This is the normal and healing reaction to sorrow and loss.

However upsetting it may be to other people to see the distress of mourners at a funeral, they should try to see also that grief and tears are natural and be glad that nature is taking a hand in the healing process.

In our society, some people have been brought up to think that it is not right to cry in public. Even though they may exercise rigid control at the funeral, they should be allowed—or perhaps encouraged—to weep in private or in sympathetic company if they need to. Boys and girls should be allowed to give full expression not only to grief but also to other strong emotions so that fear, anger, guilt and resentment can be faced and dealt with. In bereavement, expression is always better than suppression. (See the chapter *Mourning*.)

Many people find a warm drink—perhaps a cup of tea—particularly comforting. The body loses moisture through crying, so it is good to drink more than usual. Don't be afraid to take a simple painkiller such as aspirin if you get a headache from the tension. The more you take care of your physical needs the fewer problems you are likely to have.

THE WILL

As soon as possible after the death, the executors of the will should begin their task of putting its instructions into action. They should arrange to see a solicitor and ask them to obtain probate. This process is known as 'proving a will' ('Confirmation of the Will' in Scotland) and should not take more than a few weeks, depending on how complicated the will is, and on how fast the solicitor works.

In the case of a very simple estate, it is perfectly possible for a capable member of the family to deal with the matter themselves. A leaflet given by the Registrar of Deaths explains what to do.

The solicitor

The choice of solicitor is up to the executors, and they should ask him or her for a rough estimate of fees before engaging them to do the job. If the executors are not satisfied with this, they are quite at liberty to shop around.

Solicitors are there to help you, and will answer any queries you may have in terms which you can understand.

No will

Solicitors will also help you if you find that the person has, as far as you can see, died without making a will. This is termed 'intestacy'. In this situation the relatives should gather together all the information they can about what the person owned, his or her estate, and take all the documents they can find to the solicitor. There are certain rules laid down by law to cover intestacy, and usually the next of kin will inherit the estate.

Although the laws are designed to be broadly fair to surviving family members, they cannot possibly take account of individual needs. The split between a surviving spouse and the children can, for example, put the security of the family home at risk when the children come of age. A solicitor will be able to advise on how to handle the situation to avoid problems.

Other cases

Sometimes the dead person will have made their will without the help of a solicitor, usually on a form obtained from a stationer. In this case, the executors, if there are any, should take the will to a solicitor as soon as possible after the death, so that the solicitor can try to obtain probate. There are many legal pitfalls which someone making their own will may have fallen into, and it is best to have proper legal advice to help sort them out.

If you (or any close relative of the dead person) feel that you have been treated unfairly in the will, you should write to the solicitor and tell them as soon as possible (in Australia, within two months of the details being published). You may find that you can appeal to the court for the will to be changed in your favour, but you must lodge your complaint within six months of probate being granted.

How long?

If there are not too many complications, an estate can usually be wound up within six months of the death. When a business is involved it may take longer. The cost varies considerably, and will, of course, depend on how long it takes the solicitor to sort it all out. The solicitor's fee will usually come out of the estate.

Belongings

One of the most difficult tasks to tackle after a death is the disposal of the dead person's clothes and other things. It is best done soon. If you can't face it alone, ask a member of the family or a close friend to help you with it. The longer you put it off, the more you are likely to dread it.

Resist the temptation to make a 'shrine' of any place you particularly associate with the person who has died. A century ago, it was a common custom to leave everything as it had been, to behave as though the dead person would be coming back and to try to maintain a relationship which no longer existed.

Susan couldn't bear to see her husband's empty chair;

neither could she bring herself to get rid of it. One day, when her son went to see her, he said, 'Why don't you sit in it yourself, Mother?' She did and said, 'Oh, I feel really close to Fred, now.'

Geoffrey found it impossible to believe that his wife had died. He refused to get rid of anything. All her clothes remained in the drawers and wardrobe, her nightdress under her pillow, her toothbrush in the bathroom. He said it brought her closer. He felt she was 'still there'. Eventually, he was persuaded to go and stay with his son for a few weeks. When they took him home, he couldn't go into the house. 'I can't face seeing all her things,' he said. 'It will bring it all back.'

June went to the other extreme. A week after her son's funeral (he had been killed in a car crash) she systematically turned out every single thing which had belonged to him. She even tore his photographs out of frames and albums. Then she went into the garden and lit a bonfire. Weeks later, her husband found her walking in and out of all the rooms in the house, hugging herself and crying. 'There's nothing left of him. He's gone. I've got nothing to remember him by.'

Many lives have been cramped and stunted by unwise attitudes to death. By all means keep and treasure some things which have special significance and provide happy memories, but it is best to give the rest away.

There will be some items which you may want certain people to have, such as a piece of jewellery or a fountain pen, which you know they will treasure too and keep as a memento. Of the remainder, clothing, books or furniture are always needed by various voluntary organizations who will usually arrange for them to be collected.

3
Understanding Death

What is death?

Nothing perplexes us more than death. It seems a strange, unnatural disaster that makes us aware that, in the end, we have no power to control our own lives. A whole industry has grown up to try to ward off the inevitable. Millions of pounds are spent on potions and lotions, diets, exercise regimes and every sort of device to postpone it as long as possible. So, what does it mean? Why should it happen? How best can we face up to it?

The body dies

Medical science can *describe* death in a straightforward enough way. Throughout life the parts of the body continually repair themselves, but as we get older these repairs are not as successful as they used to be, and at last the vital organs break down. Similarly the body's repair systems may not be able to cope when it is harmed by disease or severe injury. The heart stops beating, breathing ceases and—the final, irreversible step—the brain no longer functions. Then life has departed and cannot be brought back.

More than a body

It is hard to believe that when the body dies the person no longer exists, though some think so. Despite the mystery of death, most people are intuitively certain that the human personality is more than just the body and that in some way we must all pass through death.

There have been many different beliefs about what actually happens. Some have thought that humans have an immortal soul which at death is freed from the hindrances of the body. Some believe that the dying person is taken into God and merged with the divine, losing their identity. Hinduism and other Eastern faiths teach reincarnation—that after death people are reborn as another baby or an animal—and so on over and over again.

The whole person—the Christian view

Christians believe that people are not simply bodies. Neither are they immortal spirits living in human bodies like snails in their shells so that at death they can discard the useless body with relief. The Christian belief is that each individual is a whole person, a unity of body, mind and spirit, and our personality is expressed through every part of our make-up.

Separation

So there *is* something unnatural about death. It separates the personality and the body, which were meant to be closely joined. And, as the bereaved know only too well, death separates you from those you love. The anguish and horror of death show that it is an enemy of human beings.

The Bible makes sense of all this by explaining that death is

---

What the Bible says about death

If our hope in Christ is good for this life only and no more, then we deserve more pity than anyone else in the world. But the truth is that Christ has been raised from death, as the guarantee that those who sleep in death will also be raised.

Our brothers, we want you to know the truth about those who have died, so that you will not be sad, as are those who have no hope. We believe that Jesus died and rose again, and so we believe that God will take back with Jesus those who have died believing in him.

Jesus said to Martha, 'I am the resurrection and the life. Whoever believes in me will live, even though he dies; and whoever lives and believes in me will never die.'

---

an aberration. It is the result of people's disobeying God, ignoring him and living their lives without him. This separation is a kind of 'death' even when they are alive. Bodily death is a further stage in what can be the final separation of a person from the God who made them.

New life in Jesus

So Christians look at death realistically and don't try to say it doesn't matter. They recognize how dreadful it is. But they also realize that they have a source of hope—Jesus Christ, the founder of Christianity.

He was executed on a cross. Death, the Bible explains, is the normal consequence of humanity's disobedience to God; but Jesus took the punishment on himself, on behalf of all people.

But there is more: when Jesus rose again from death it was to a new life in which anyone can share if they put their trust in him. Because that new life is imperishable, death is now a gateway to an even closer friendship with God. It is a deep comfort to those left behind to know that death can't separate them for ever from those who have died. Because of Christ, they will be reunited.

The resurrection of the body

The Christian idea of heaven is not a place where immortal souls float around! After all, Jesus himself was raised from death physically, with a real body, not as a ghost. Christians believe that when this world's time is up, the bodies of all who have died will be raised. Individuals will be judged by God as whole people, and believers will have an unimaginably full life with God for ever.

No longer unbearable

And so death loses its terror for those who believe the Christian good news. It is still solemn, and undeniably sad, but Christian hope makes it bearable. This isn't wishful thinking, either, for it is based on God's strength and love which he demonstrated by raising Jesus from the dead.

4
Coping with Grief

It is perfectly normal for a bereaved person to be sad, withdrawn and tearful. It does not mean that he or she is depressive or neurotic. Normal human experiences cannot simply be written off as medical problems.

Grief is like an illness, though, and can be disabling. Sometimes the bereaved person is affected by physical symptoms, often similar to the ones which had afflicted the dead person, and these should not be ignored, although almost always they disappear after a week or two. No matter how 'sensible' we imagine ourselves to be, our emotional behaviour after the loss of someone close to us seems puzzling and frightening. It is possible to remain dry-eyed and apparently unmoved at the funeral and yet be intensely affected by very little things.

THE PATTERN

After the first, numbing shock, there comes a period of pining. This is followed by mixed feelings of depression and apathy which alternate with bursts of intense activity and, often, anger and despair.

How long?

Many mourners have cried, 'How long will it last?' It is impossible to generalize. Within reason, any length of time is 'normal'. Such a fundamental adjustment has to be a gradual process. A very rough estimate would be a year or two, while we learn to accept what has happened and to adapt to the situation. After, say, two years, a drawn-out, disabling grief suggests that medical help should be sought. Such a problem will be familiar to a doctor and they will be

Timetable of grief

(This description of grief is very general. The stages and their order vary, and may overlap.)

First stage

1 Shock
Muscular weakness, emptiness and inner tension

2 Numbness
Everything seems unreal and remote

Second stage

3 Struggle between fantasy and reality
You find reality difficult to accept and may act partly as though it had not happened

4 Feelings of guilt, panic or frenzy
You may want to withdraw from the outside world and even your family

5 Anxiety

6 Anger

7 Bitterness

8 Other symptoms

Third stage

9 Tears
Shedding of tears or a release of a flood of grief

10 Painful memories
You find yourself able to face memories and accept them

11 Acceptance
Your new life begins and plans for the future form. Practical and emotional problems become easier to deal with.

able to suggest ways in which the bereaved person can gradually overcome this depressive stage.

What about the children?

If your children are in need of more support than you can give them at the moment, then ask the health visitor to call, and perhaps your local authority social worker. They will be able to advise on day nurseries or put you in touch with a registered child-minder.

It is better to be occupied than to sit about and worry. It will help the children if they are allowed to give a hand with any job they can do. To do things together gives everyone a sense of purpose and security. In all times of grief, habit can be a comfort—to go on doing the daily chores, peeling the potatoes, going to work, going to school, and the like. To pick up the day-to-day threads of life as soon as possible will give you all a feeling of competence, however tentative, that you will be able to cope with the situation.

Understanding yourself

Any one who has experienced bereavement can fully understand its conflicting emotions. You are over-sensitive to casual remarks; you dread waking up in the morning, especially at weekends when you imagine everyone else is having a good time. Everything becomes out of proportion: nothing seems as important as your own grief.

You are amazed and frightened by the intensity of emotions you never knew you had or that you had always been able to suppress. A middle-aged widow who had imagined herself as competent, controlled and self-sufficient, found to her dismay that some days she became 'a trembly bag of bones', as she put it, paralyzed with fear at the thought of doing the most simple and familiar jobs. A high-powered senior civil servant, supremely self-confident in his ability to control everything that came his way, admitted feelings of deep shame that, in a moment of panic, he had rung up a colleague in the middle of the night and asked him to talk for a little while.

One of the main effects of bereavement is a restless desire to be 'doing something'. This restlessness comes from the instinct to look for the dead person; disbelief that he or she has really gone. One woman who went back to work and managed well during the week found at weekends that she needlessly turned out drawers, swept out the garage, rearranged the furniture, before a friend suggested to her that she was trying to 'find' her dead husband.

Some try to 'bring back' the loved one by way of fantasies or speaking aloud to them as though they were in the room. Some experience vivid dreams; many of these recall happy events in the past but most have an underlying uneasiness, complicated by the conflicting need to find the dead person and the fear of actually doing so.

Vivid memories

Equally common is the sharply-defined recollection of the events which led up to the death and the ability of the bereaved to recount every detail of the previous hours and days. It is as though time stood still, just as a single moment is captured in a photograph.

You remember that it was the day the mail was late or the day you missed the bus to work. One man, months later, was able to recite word for word a letter he had just read when the news of his wife's death was brought to him. Bereaved people will hang on to such details as a means of making their dead seem closer and still with them in the world. It is as though, if they could make time stand still, it wouldn't have happened. Or, after something dreadful has happened, for a few seconds you wish it was still yesterday.

Finding your way

We react differently to bereavement according to our temperament, our upbringing, the people we are with, and other less obvious causes. Some long to talk to anyone who will listen; others shut themselves away and talk within themselves; others will write it all down in the form of a diary or a letter to the one who has died. One of the best known examples of this is the book C.S. Lewis wrote after his wife died, *A Grief Observed*, extracts of which are often quoted and his reactions recognized by anyone who has been bereaved.

There is no 'right' way of grieving—everyone has to work a way through by whatever method brings most relief and comfort. Although we can derive much help and insight from other people's experiences, in the end we all have to fight our own way through the jungle, making use of every bit of encouragement we can find.

THE FIRST STAGE OF GRIEF

The trouble is—we don't know what to expect! If death has never before come so close, bereavement is a new experience and we don't know how to deal with it. A book like this can help by trying to explain what is happening and describing the emotions which are tearing you apart. Whatever your emotions may be, never be afraid of your own reactions to grief. Accept them, try to understand them, and you will be halfway to using them positively.

Shock

Your first reaction is likely to be one of shock. You may feel yourself 'go to jelly', or as if you no longer fit together. You find it hard to relate to the world around you.

Numbness

Be thankful for the numbness which carries you through the first days or weeks, even though you know that feeling is bound to return—like the pain in frost-bitten fingers when they begin to thaw.

If possible, use this short break, when often the mind works clearly and competently on a practical level, to cope with the immediate problems, and thus prevent yourself losing confidence in your ability to manage on your own. But you should try not to make any far-reaching decisions until much later: in your present state of mind your judgment will not be reliable. Refuse to be pressured by anyone, however close to you and well-meaning, into doing anything which may not be possible to reverse when you may be feeling differently about your future.

SECOND STAGE

The struggle between fantasy and reality

This is when many irrational fears and emotions come to the surface. These are entirely natural. People often feel physically ill, fear they are going mad or think they are about to have a nervous breakdown. As they struggle to control the conflict inside them, all sorts of dreadful possibilities run through their minds. None of these imaginary disasters is likely to happen. When this stage hit me, I found it helpful to try to imagine what *I* would say to someone in the same situation and then say it to myself. It is always easy to give someone else advice and to see things from one step removed but it did give a sort of proportion to imaginings which had got out of hand.

Guilt, panic and frenzy

In the mental and emotional turmoil, it is hard to keep hold of reality. Many fears may then creep in. One of the greatest fears a bereaved person may have is that they will also die.

I myself feared that this would happen to me, leaving the children orphaned. Again, I made myself think of people who had died and how many of their spouses had followed them within days or weeks and I couldn't name a single one. My mother (who had herself been widowed less than a year before) used to say, as she had when I was a child, 'Now you're just being fanciful; such silly ideas!' That no-nonsense approach might not work for everyone but I had been brought up on it and it helped me!

Anxiety

It is quite natural for you to feel that you cannot cope, and that the problems and worries of everyday life are threatening to overwhelm you. Try to live one day at a time, and not to look too far into the future. If you are seriously over-anxious, it is worthwhile exploring the various relaxation techniques which reduce both physical tension and mental agitation. Ask your doctor or health visitor for information.

The Bible has some sound advice for dealing with anxiety:

> *So do not worry about tomorrow; it will have enough worries of its own. There is no need to add to the troubles each day brings.*
> THE GOSPEL OF MATTHEW

> *Don't worry about anything, but in all your prayers ask God for what you need, always asking him with a*

thankful heart. And God's peace, which is far beyond human understanding, will keep your hearts and minds safe in union with Christ Jesus.
PAUL'S LETTER TO THE PHILIPPIANS

Anger

One emotion which upsets and shocks many people is a feeling of extreme anger. Anger frequently goes with fear; an animal may be docile until something frightens it, when it will turn and attack, or a parent may smack a child who has run into the road because fear has turned to anger.

For the bereaved person, the world has suddenly become a very frightening place, and one reaction is to fight back. Most people blame themselves in some measure for the death of someone near to them, and because this is too painful to bear they tend to take it out on someone else. I still feel ashamed that when the milkman called for his money at the end of the week, I shouted at him for making me come to the door for anything so trivial.

Bereaved people will find many scapegoats on which to unload their anger. One woman marched into her husband's office and accused his colleagues of not pulling their weight and leaving him to shoulder all the responsibility. Another blamed her doctor for making what she considered had been a wrong diagnosis of the person who had died.

Life seems very unjust. Many blame God. 'How can he love us if he lets this happen?' they ask. 'What have we done to deserve this?' There is no need to feel guilty for voicing such thoughts. When doctors are the subject of wild accusations after bereavement, they do not let it affect their relationship with the patient.

How much greater is God's understanding of our turmoil! Speaking as a Christian, I believe that the greatest comfort we have is to know that we can take all our fears, resentment and anger to him, believing that such destructive emotions will gradually be healed by his love to be replaced by peace and hope. We don't become immune from tragedy if we believe in God, but we can be protected from bitterness and despair in our suffering by his strength and presence with us.

Bitterness

Bitterness is a destructive emotion which we must guard against. If we become bitter it will set up hostilities within the family on account of the cruel, unjust things we shall say. This is a time when we should be drawing strength from being united, but, sadly, it can also be a time when relationships are damaged beyond repair. We have all heard people say, 'I do think they might have...' or 'I shall never forgive her for...' or 'I gave up everything to look after Dad and now...' I had read about this emotion after bereavement and remember praying almost at once, 'Please, God, don't let me be bitter.'

It should not be necessary to point out that a child must never, even by implication, be blamed for contributing to the death of a parent or of a brother or sister. That would be too much to bear when he or she is already suffering his or her personal grief.

For the same reason, it is thoughtless as well as stupid to vent one's anger on a close friend or relative. All the time we have to guard against situations developing which, for the sake of relieving our tension, alienate people who want to help. Of *course* we shall sometimes lose our temper and lash out often on those we love most but, if this happens, we must be quick to apologize and to heal any wound we have caused.

Mary knew the wisdom of this after she had reduced her daughter-in-law to tears by her bitter words. She put her arms around her and said, 'I'm sorry. I didn't mean it. It wasn't even true. I just had to blame *someone* for everything I was feeling!'

Other symptoms

Sometimes, the bereaved will notice physical symptoms; these symptoms normally fade within a week or so without producing the real illness from which the dead person had suffered.

The day after my husband's funeral, I went to my doctor because one side of my face was swollen and inflamed and I was sure that I had caught the same disease. The doctor

Destructive attitudes	Constructive attitudes
◇ bitterness	◇ accepting what has happened
◇ despair	◇ hopefulness
◇ pride	◇ faith in the future
◇ shutting yourself away	◇ making the most of what is left
◇ self-pity	
◇ looking for someone to blame	◇ willingness to recover
	◇ being thankful for the past
◇ becoming a martyr	◇ accepting help and friendship
◇ cursing God	◇ committing everything to God

assured me that I was perfectly healthy and that my face would soon return to normal. It did.

A young husband whose wife had died in pregnancy suffered for several days what could only be described as labour pains.

Many women who have lost a husband as a result of heart disease imagine that they are about to go the same way, not realizing that quickened heart-beats or palpitations are often the response to fear and anxiety.

The only thing which saves us from hypochondria is a sense of humour. Try to see the funny side of your reactions. I have thanked God for the laughter of family and friends.

Another disconcerting effect of bereavement is a form of illusion in which we 'see' the dead person. This can be so vivid that we find ourselves reaching out to touch or call out to them. This is all the more frightening because we know that hallucinations can be a symptom of insanity. We need to be reassured that they are no more than a normal after-effect of loss.

But it can be an agonizing disappointment to walk along a street, sure that the person in front is your dead relative. It may be just a way of walking, but the jolt is enough to pierce the heart and bring back all the pain. The hallucinatory phase is heightened if the bereaved person possesses a very clear visual memory which is triggered off by any resemblance to the dead person in someone else.

Maggie had to fight her unwillingness to go into the town because she kept 'seeing' her dead brother in every Ford Transit van that passed her. Widows who have nursed their husband through a long illness frequently get up at night because they 'hear' him coughing.

All this can be difficult for other people to understand and, as at so many other times, I found the only person I could turn to was Jesus, who had wept over the death of his friend Lazarus and who knows what sadness and grief are like. A Christian friend of mine found much consolation in contemplating how Mary must have felt after witnessing the crucifixion and her subsequent grief, bewilderment and disturbing memories.

THE THIRD STAGE

Tears
Letting go of our dead is the most difficult and yet the most

---

Every bereaved person will experience some of the following physical and emotional symptoms:

◇ insomnia

◇ trembling

◇ coldness

◇ indigestion

◇ constipation

◇ coughs and colds

◇ lapses of memory

◇ fatigue

◇ loss of appetite

◇ lack of concentration

◇ itching skin

◇ blurred vision

◇ difficulty in swallowing

◇ nervousness

◇ depression

◇ panic

◇ anxiety

◇ sweating

◇ fear of illness

◇ fear of breakdown

◇ headaches

◇ dizziness

◇ diarrhoea

◇ irritability

◇ lack of interest

◇ fullness in the throat

---

important part of grief and mourning. Gradually we have to cut those ties which hold us back from making a new life for ourselves and the family. We must slowly wean ourselves away from negative ideas and actions adopted in the first weeks or months of bereavement, from self-defensive rituals which may become too entrenched to relinquish, even when we know they are no longer helpful. Memories must remain and be a source of comfort and thankfulness, but if we refuse to accept the fact of death we shall become stunted, unable to grow—surely this would not be what those who loved us would want to happen.

In the past, it was the custom for the bereaved person or family to make regular visits to the grave, to replace dead flowers or to kneel in silence. For some this was a necessary observance and a source of comfort, for others it was a dreaded duty which made matters worse. Studies have shown that cremation, in most cases, helps the bereaved to let go more easily and quickly.

Painful memories

Mercifully, the true realization of what we have lost comes only slowly, but each day will bring its reminders of the past. This pervading sadness was summed up by one widow who said, 'I keep thinking I must tell Jim about that when he gets home—and then I remember that I shan't be able to tell him anything ever again.'

Different associations bring pain to different people. A widower never set foot in his local pub after his wife died because they had always had their Saturday lunch there when she was alive. Another man wrote to his vicar and told him he intended joining another church because he felt he would always 'see' his wife in the pew they had always occupied, and he felt he must begin a new church life in a different building.

Although I can hardly believe now that it took so long, my diary tells me that it was four years before I could listen to a record or go to a concert. I do remember, though, that the tears which accompanied the music when I did feel able to hear it again were peaceful rather than painful, and I knew that another stage of my own mourning had passed.

If you have lived with someone for a long time, it makes it all the more difficult to take decisions and make changes you know your loved one would probably have disapproved of or disliked. There was a man I used to visit; his wife had recently died and his sons wanted him to have a television set. 'No,' he said, 'Emmy didn't approve of television.' Nothing would move him. Unfortunately, Emmy hadn't been too keen on the radio, either, so his evenings must have been long and lonely. However, in the end he was persuaded to have a set, though obviously feeling very guilty about it.

Acceptance

To accept what has happened demands two things—time and the willingness to recover. You have to learn how much you can take at a time. There is nothing so tiring as strong emotion and the bereaved person is often very tired indeed. You must learn how much you can bear of the company of certain people, well-meaning though they may be. Recognize what situations you cannot face just yet—it was at least two years before I could go to a funeral. Faced with a painful situation, it is prudent not to ask too much of yourself and when you do venture into something stressful, to try to provide yourself with an escape route such as 'I'll sit at the back so that I can go out', or 'I'll ask someone to come with me.' Do not push yourself. Above all, never feel inadequate or defeated when you have to give in for a while.

Some days you feel more able to do things than others, so it is only sensible to press ahead then and not to attempt too much on the bad days. This gradual adjustment to life will enable you to regain your balance and perspective. The numb period at the beginning of mourning gives the needed breathing-space to come to terms with changed circumstances. Realization dawns slowly, different aspects become more clear, the future begins to shape itself and is often shaped by outside events. Look at each new problem squarely and deal with it only when it happens—not before.

Within the family, all the members can help each other. How about encouraging each other to laugh in, and at, some situations?

IS THERE ANYBODY THERE?

It is easy to understand why the savage separation which death brings makes some people turn to spiritualism in an effort to make contact with the ones they have lost. Every bereaved person longs to speak to them just once more and to know if they are 'all right'. The reactions of those who have consulted a medium or gone to a spiritualist church are mixed. Some have felt that a contact *has* been made, others have felt frightened, others disappointed that 'nothing happened' or that any 'messages' have been almost insultingly trivial.

To my mind, this desire to make contact reveals a selfish element in our love. Instead of letting them go, we are trying to bind them to an earthly existence when they have been set free to continue their journey in a new place and time-scale. Instead of allowing them to go forward, we are trying to hold them back. Is it really love or is it self-concern on our part? Are we putting our sorrow before their new opportunities?

For a Christian, this attempt to keep them here on earth, where we know what is going on, shows a lack of trust in a loving God. Christians believe that he is Father of us all and loves us all equally and far more completely than we can ever love each other. We can safely commit our dead into his loving care, remembering that he has also promised strength and guidance for those who are left behind. We need fear neither for them nor for ourselves.

This may sound all very well in theory but is no defence against the pangs of grief and mourning we shall all suffer. But we need not suffer alone; God bears our cross with us as, in Jesus, he bore *his* cross *for* us. As we travel through our agony, he is in it with us so that we gradually begin to see that the end of the way will be joy. And joy is stronger than suffering because beyond the cross lies the resurrection.

DO YOU WANT TO RECOVER?

When we lose someone we have loved deeply and relied on, life loses most of its purpose. All our emotional energies are directed towards grieving for that person and our own loss. We are knocked sideways, unable to face the world. But sooner or later we have to make a fresh start, even if we cannot see where we are going. The longer the period of mourning has been, the more courage it will take to risk being hurt by life again.

Some people take refuge in 'I don't feel very well' or 'no one would want me!' Others, having become used to sympathy, forbearance and—dare I say it?—the limelight, find they do not want to rejoin the rat race.

Turning-points

Another obstacle which some people find at the start of their new life is a sense of disloyalty to the dead person. They feel it is wrong when they occasionally experience a shaft of joy. They feel ashamed when they find they have forgotten their grief when they are with friends. The morning after an evening out with her daughter and son-in-law, Dorothy woke up feeling so guilty that she had 'forgotten' Bill for a few hours that she was unable to go out of the house and forced herself back into a pattern of grieving and mourning from which she had just begun to emerge. This, of course, perplexed and worried her daughter and made her inhibited about suggesting any other diversion.

But a slow coming back into the world is how it should be. After all, your partner or relative wasn't at the forefront of your mind every minute of every day when they were alive; neither should they be now. These times of forgetting, happiness even, are to be welcomed. They show that true healing is well under way.

One woman said she knew the worst was over when she went up to the loft to check that the lagging round the tank was in place before the winter, without even thinking that this was a job her husband would have done.

Slowly, the piercing pain of grief will give place to the

dull ache of mourning and then to lengthening periods of calm when memories bring more happiness than sorrow. You will know, then, that all is well. We are encouraged to notice this sign within members of the family. David came home from school some months after his father's death and told his mother, 'I was sad when I remembered that Dad wouldn't be there to see me bat but then I forgot all about him and made sixty-three.' His mother wisely said, 'That's just as Dad would have wanted it.'

Taking stock

This is the time to take stock.

○ consider new interests

○ get in touch with old friends

○ make plans—however restricted they may have to be

○ don't make loneliness a way of life—that would be a poor tribute to the person you have lost

Take stock of yourself, as well. Respect your body and mind when they tell you you have overdone things. If you are tired, have a rest and do the chores later. If you are holding down a job and keeping the family together, don't be too proud to accept any offer of help during the week so that you will have more time to spend with the children at the weekend. Try to make some time each day for yourself when you do whatever *you* want to do which raises your self-esteem. It may be a leisurely bath or a sit down with a new book or half-an-hour's gardening or a pub lunch with a friend—and no qualms about being 'selfish'!

There will still come days when nothing seems worthwhile, or there's no one to do anything for, or you think 'Who cares, anyway?' It helped me to recall the medieval philosophy that the smallest thing done well—arranging a vase of flowers, carving a piece of wood, weeding a flower-bed—anything which adds to the goodness and beauty of the world, satisfies the worker and gives glory to the Creator.

5
Mourning

Grief is what we experience after bereavement: mourning is the way in which we express it. Mourning is of the utmost importance because it is the working out of grief. To bottle it up is a great mistake. Feelings not acknowledged do not go away and if buried may erupt many years later with devastating effect.

RITUALS AND CONVENTIONS

Until the early part of this century, the whole community would be affected by a death. Blinds were drawn in the house of the bereaved family and in the windows of houses along the route taken by the funeral procession. Black crêpe ribbons hung on the doors. When the hearse passed by, people stood still or raised their hats and lowered their eyes. Relatives dressed in black, used black-edged paper for their letters, wore veils in public, stayed indoors for a time and cancelled all social engagements for several months. Society recognized that mourners were people with a special role in the life of the community.

Security

Much of this seems to us, now, an excessive and morbid attitude to death, but it had its advantages. The mourners knew what was expected of them and it gave them security in a world which had tumbled about their ears. They knew the part they had to play, and as the prescribed period of mourning slipped away, so, usually, did their own grief.

A definite pattern of mourning was comforting to conform to and in most cases it 'worked'. Gradual physical emergence into the world again coincided with gradual emotional emergence as well. The rites and customs had been observed; life could continue. They were protected by the conventions. I remember an uncle, a des-perately shy man, devastated by the death of his wife, apparently having no difficulty in walking down the road a day or two after her funeral. 'I shall go to the Post Office with these letters,' he said, 'and no one will stop me or speak to me.'

The modern taboo

Today, we are less willing to face the fact of death. True, certain rituals are observed, at least in the first few days. We write to the family concerned, send flowers, ask if we can do anything to help. Then we try to dismiss the whole subject from our minds—it strikes too near home and makes us fear for ourselves.

The modern attitude to grief makes it much more difficult to mourn adequately. We have been indoctrinated with the idea that to mourn for longer than a week or two shows a weakness of will, if not sheer self-indulgence. Because death is nowadays a forbidden subject, it is more difficult to impress on those who do not understand that, far from being morbid or thoughtless, mourning is a psychological necessity.

Grief may be suppressed in many ways. Some people will keep themselves over-busy, never letting up or relaxing, gearing themselves up to a punishing pace. Some will try to carry on exactly as before, giving themselves no time to think or adjust. Some will throw themselves into a round of social activity and affect a brittle brightness. Others keep themselves under a rigid control, not letting go even when alone. The resultant physical, mental and emotional strain will, in the end, be too stressful to keep up and something will snap. In these situations, 'Aren't they being wonderful?' is not necessarily a compliment.

Going to the funeral

The funeral is the last service (in both senses) that we do for our dead, but I believe it is of even greater service to the living. It is distressing to see the grief of those who mourn, but the sympathy of neighbours and the respect for grief has tremendous value in supporting the bereaved within a comforting framework of convention.

The vast majority of mourners derive much consolation from the service itself. The words seem to stick in their minds and come back to them in the weeks that follow.

A widower told the minister after his wife's funeral, 'It said all the things I couldn't say myself.'

A widow explained how surprised she had been to see so many in church: 'I felt so proud of him ... all those people ... they must have thought the world of him.'

Another said, 'I looked round and there were all my friends. For the first time, I didn't feel alone.'

It also ties up the loose ends of the life which is over; it reassures us that we have done everything necessary on a practical plane.

'We gave him a good send-off, didn't we?' was how one widow put it. 'It tidies everything up,' said another. 'Now I feel I can start again—a bit like Monday morning.'

This 'tidying up' is an important start to the grieving process. The old life has fallen apart; nothing will be the same again. But rituals and observances are the scaffolding within which the framework of the next stage of life can be built. They provide both a safety net and a jumping-off ground.

SIGHING AND CRYING

There's nothing like a good cry. Sighing and crying are the most obvious and most understandable expressions of grief, and doctors agree that if we repress these two outlets, or are denied them by others, we are more likely to become disturbed later on.

This is borne out by the case of a man who showed no outward sign of grief after his wife's death but some years later, after visiting her sick sister in the same hospital, suffered a nervous breakdown.

There are many reasons for tears and they are not always

simply for the dead person. There are also the tears of fear and helplessness—as when Margaret banged her fists on the table and shouted, 'Where are you, Bob? I *need* you.' There are the tears of anger: 'How could you leave me?' There are the tears of guilt: 'I knew she was ill but I got so fed up with it all and kept losing my temper with her.' There are the tears of regret: 'If only I'd rung up more often or taken the children over sometimes. Now it's too late.' And there are the tears of self-pity: these, too, are natural and normal but must be recognized for what they are and not allowed to become destructive rather than healing.

Natural sorrow

For a while, we have to let ourselves down lightly and not fight to keep up appearances or conform to attitudes demanded by modern society.

At times of international conflict, as well as in the aftermath of more domestic tragedies, we have all seen pictures of people sobbing uncontrollably, their faces crumpled and twisted by the intensity of their grief. Many people feel that it is wrong to show such scenes, that outsiders should not be witness to such naked grief. Often, media coverage *is* an intrusion but I still think it is necessary to understand that the bereaved *should* cry and give full expression to their feelings. It is part of the 'work' of mourning and will help them come through it to the other side.

Conventions

But not everyone is able to let themselves go in this way. Older people, brought up in times when it was considered bad taste to show any strong emotion, will often hold themselves on a very tight rein.

I was recently at the funeral of an elderly man; his widow was quietly crying and her sister leaned across and said loudly, 'Stop it, Elizabeth, everyone's looking at you.' Later, that widow bitterly resented the fact that even more attention had been focused on her and had made it impossible for her to 'take the funeral in'.

Barriers

Mourners who suffer most are those who are surrounded by relatives or friends with whom they cannot be natural. Some parents find it impossible to talk about the death with their children; some feel, mistakenly, that the children must be shielded from grief. This is made more difficult if the children themselves are unwilling or unable to speak about their dead parent or grandparent. A situation arises where no one knows what to do because no one knows what would be helpful.

In these cases, a friend or relative can often break the silence so that everyone can be natural. Some mourners cannot turn to their elderly parents for help because they don't want to upset them. Some have quarrelled with their parents or their in-laws and have no point of contact with them any more. Those who are mourning the death of a parent or grandparent may feel that there is no one to turn to. Ironically, the relative who has died may well be the one who would have provided comfort in the situation.

Your own expectations

Many women have fought long and hard to establish a reputation for self-sufficiency and competence in a world that has been suspicious if not downright dismissive of their abilities. They dare not, even in the face of death, 'let themselves down' as they call it, or admit that they are not invincible or possessed of unassailable self-control.

Others feel that it is proper for women to weep prettily. These people may be distressed if—as may easily happen—their tears are more emotional than seems appropriate. Yet others may feel they have acted wrongly if they do not cry at times when people 'expect' them to.

Men can be particularly hard hit in bereavement because of the traditional 'stiff upper lip' attitude which most have been taught to assume. To this day few allow themselves to cry in public. Many feel they cannot do so even within the family and suffer accordingly. One young widower with sons of ten and eight said, 'I mustn't give way. What would they think?' I've always told them that only babies cry.' But boys, in particular, benefit from seeing their father's tears.

Imagine the conflict in a lad who imagines it is sissy to cry and yet whose most urgent need is to release his desperation in this way. He may well be surprised, even shocked, to see his own father cry, but he will also learn that there is nothing wrong in the natural expression of grief and that tears at such a time have dignity and worth. Father and son can then grieve together and comfort each other.

Each person and family will have their own ways of coping with their common grief and no way is more 'right' than another if it brings relief at the crucial time.

When June died, Peter and his three young children found it easier to cry together: the whole family had been used to speaking openly on all sorts of subjects. 'We're crying because we're sad and we all miss Mummy so much,' he explained. 'After all, she wouldn't like to think we didn't care.'

If you repress every emotion, you create a barrier around yourself which no one can penetrate. It shuts you in and keeps other people out. You condemn yourself to suffer alone—and that is loneliness indeed.

Solidarity

The same expressions of grief which can drive people away from those who mourn can also be a means of drawing together those chiefly concerned. Children should be allowed to join in the emotions of bereaved parents. In the early stages, tears come frequently and unexpectedly, but soon a pattern of recovery begins to form—the one who stops crying first comforts the others and you all continue with the task in hand.

On a particularly bad day after my husband died when we were all crying at once, I remember one of the boys eventually blowing his nose and saying, 'There, I'm better now. I'll go and make some coffee.'

6
What Will It Mean?

WHO AM I?

We all need someone to love who loves us, and when a close relationship is broken we feel painfully alone. A widow who lost her husband, her mother and her sister, all within a year, explained, 'I don't feel special any more. I miss being cherished.'

Many people who have enjoyed a close relationship with another person derive great support from their companionship, whatever form it takes. If one of them dies, part of their own 'life support' dies with them. Self-confidence, security and even identity are hurt.

LOSS OF YOUR ROLE

The psychological afflictions need to be dealt with promptly. One bewildered woman said, 'You feel as though you were in a train which has gone on and left you in a siding.'

Paul, aged thirteen, complained, 'I feel as though the TV's been switched off and I've been left on "hold".'

Your role in life has changed. It might seem quite a subtle shift: if, as a grown-up, you lose an elderly parent who lived far away, you may find little change in your daily routine. Nevertheless, the passing of the generation ahead of you makes you feel older, more aware of your own mortality. You need time to adjust to this new view of yourself. This is even more true if you lose a parent or grandparent you were close to. Not only are you 'pushed up' a generation, but there is an acute sense of the loss of their presence and companionship.

Partnership is an especially close relationship, and the loss of a partner presents unique challenges. Indeed, the Christian marriage service speaks of husband and wife being 'one flesh', so it is hardly surprising that a bereaved spouse feels that half of them is missing.

Younger children, too, will be aware that something about their role has changed: the shape of their family is different. It may cause only a small change—perhaps their contact with a grandparent was limited to occasional visits—or it may dramatically affect the household, especially if a parent dies.

For all these reasons, bereavement can bring an acute sense of isolation. Who now will listen as you talk out the problems of the day, the plans for the future? It seems impossible that another relationship of the same quality will ever be forged. Worse, it seems that you will forever feel bereft.

Something bereaved people have to guard against is getting used to living on the edge of other people's lives, reading about and listening to what everyone else is doing but taking no steps to join in, feeling that they now have no part to play in normal living. But this must change. Your steps towards forging a new role for yourself will present many challenges.

Doing the other person's work

Many family relationships exist within a framework of sharing: a wife may be in charge of home decoration, a father may maintain the garden, a grandparent may cook Sunday lunch for the whole tribe, a child may be responsible for the family pet. So it is quite unnerving when the bereaved have to tackle 'their' jobs for the first time.

In the early days of my widowhood, I felt guilty about opening letters addressed to my husband and some days found myself putting them on one side 'for when he comes home'. Other days, I used to stare at the envelopes and think, 'Who is Mr V.B. Richardson? He doesn't exist.'

In the case of older couples who have become almost dependent on their partner, fear may assume panic proportions. Faced with a letter from the bank asking for instructions over some standing orders, one woman broke down, shivering and sobbing, 'I don't know. I always asked Charles before I wrote a cheque or signed anything.' She had to be assured that there are always people to give advice and organizations that will help. (See the list in the chapter *Preparing For Bereavement.*)

In addition to the problem of doing jobs that the other did is the problem of doing single-handedly tasks that were always shared: be it raking up autumn leaves, getting the shopping home, tousling with the children at bathtime, or driving long journeys.

With new and unfamiliar work to do, you may well feel at a loss. It takes courage even to ask for help. Yet you should do just this whenever you need to: all kinds of people around you can provide the expertise and the energy that you need, and help you find longer-term solutions to the challenges.

Handling your emotions

It is surprising how like a teenager you feel as a result of bereavement. There are the same unpredictable moods, the same periods of lethargy followed by bouts of over-activity, the same enthusiasms which fizzle out, the same hopes drowned in the same despairs.

Other bereaved people have told me that they felt humiliated by such juvenile emotions and fought them violently.

In the same way that an adolescent isn't always sure where they fit in, the bereaved person finds it difficult to decide into which age-group they fall. This is especially true of the middle-aged. You haven't the same footing as your parents' generation, of true 'seniority' in society; yet you are out of touch with young people still enthusiastically achieving 'firsts' in terms of home, career and family: first promotion, first house, first child, and so on.

If you have lost a partner, you question whether you now fit best with single people or other couples. If a parent, you may feel that you should relate to an older generation now.

I remember that, from the day when I became a widow (and the mere word is inhibiting), I felt thirty years older than my contemporaries—as though I had been catapulted into the older generation.

Humiliations

Society gets used to treating individuals as parts of their family unit. When the family changes because of bereavement, other people are as confused by the change of status. In their embarrassment, they can inflict many humiliations.

A widow is only half a pair—she makes an uneven number at table; she tends to stick out like a sore thumb; she may have to be fetched or taken home; worst of all still, she acts as a constant reminder that any of those with her may find themselves in her position one day.

A young orphan can become the object of pity: the only one not to have a personal cheerleader at the school sport's day, the one whose surviving parent can rarely—if ever—turn up to support a school function.

Grown-ups who lose their parents, particularly if they are the first of their peers to be bereaved in this way, can feel lonely and left out when their contemporaries are still busy—with trips 'back home' at Christmas, and so on.

In order to survive the slights and thoughtless suggestions which will probably come your way, it is essential to cultivate a sense of humour. A friend told me, 'Some people I know will cross the road rather than say hello—it's as though I had turned into an alien life form.'

Another widow described how she swung between laughter and tears when a well-meaning neighbour asked, 'Are you feeling better, now?' as though she was getting over a nasty attack of flu.

Neglected or suspected

Fears that you may be forgotten or written off are not without foundation. Subtle prejudices that people would deny emerge in what they do.

My experience as a widow provides telling examples. A

widow tends to be asked round for a cup of tea rather than to supper, on the grounds that 'you won't want to be out after dark'.

I felt I was now deemed fit only for female company: there is a widespread suspicion that all widows are husband-hunting. The sudden loss of masculine company is a deprivation for widows of all ages. I missed the gossip of my loved one's world and hearing the names of people whom I might not actually have met but which were part of our life together. One of the more bizarre panic feelings I had in the first few weeks was 'I don't know what's going on in the City or whether that deal went through.'

One of the difficulties of losing a parent, and more often a grandparent, is that people don't understand the impact it has had on your life. The pain of loss is intensified when friends and colleagues ask, 'Were you close?' Having to explain or justify your grief can hurt very badly.

At a time when nerve-endings are raw and exposed, it isn't easy to be brave and make yourself vulnerable to heartache, the unexpected twist of the knife. Like it or not, however, it is essential to fight your way back into your circle of friends. But we must make allowances for those who cannot possibly understand what bereavement means... yet. We must learn to laugh at the ridiculous side of many situations in which we find ourselves.

Starting from zero

Any form of deep suffering makes or breaks us. The experience of millions who have been through it is that when we feel most broken, that is the point from which we can start again. John Bunyan wrote, 'He that is down need fear no fall, he that is low no pride.' Every bereaved person is diminished—as John Donne said, 'No man is an island, entire of itself'. However, we must let ourselves be built up again.

YOUR SOCIAL LIFE

The chief emotion of anyone meeting a bereaved person for the first time is one of acute embarrassment. They don't want to upset you and they don't know what to say. Above all, they dread a public display of tears. In the past, many of us will have felt the same, so we can understand their wariness.

Making the first move

We learn that, hard though it is, it may well be up to us to make the first move. *We* have to be the ones to go up to an acquaintance in the supermarket and say hello. Once the ice has been broken, we no longer find ourselves playing hide and seek and we can talk more normally.

News will get round that you have neither been struck dumb nor made mentally deficient! Some people will be over-bracing and treat you as they would a child recovering from mumps. Some will speak in hushed voices and urge you to rest. But everyone means well and is doing their best—our part is to be grateful and to help them out.

Starting again is an exhausting business. Now, it's you who have to make all the running to keep in touch with people. If you have lost a close family member—a partner, a dependent child—your social contacts may change. The bereaved parent may no longer need to make the trip to school each day, where invitations to call round were typically offered; the bereaved partner may no longer be part of a social scene based on the other's work. It becomes a battle to see yourself as a person in your own right, and to persuade others to do so.

Join in

Gradually, you will receive invitations again. However little you feel like accepting them, make the effort because otherwise people's embarrassment will soon turn to boredom, and you may not be asked again. Go along, smile and join in.

This is all the more important if you have young children. They, too, may feel reluctant to be among 'whole' families but their life, too, must not be artificially restricted or an impression given that they want to be left out of normal socializing. The last thing a child may want is to be a special case or to appear different. One of my sons, faced with a party invitation, said to me, 'I'd like to go, but could it be just for a little while and then you come and fetch me?'

Little by little, enjoyment will replace the anguish of going without the support of the person who has died, and when you actually ask someone to come for a meal, you will know that another hurdle is over and you are beginning to find your feet again. It will take courage to return alone to an empty house or sleeping children, and no one to talk over the evening with. But we have to make the choice— either to face the world on its own terms or become a forgotten recluse.

Simple entertaining

I have heard many bereaved people explain that they can no longer have friends round now that they will have to sustain the conversation without the usual support. I suspect that is an excuse rather than a reason! As a first step, why not ask someone who has been a particular help to you to come and share a meal? You need not put on anything special.

If you are part of a family with children, you'll probably find that they love to help in the preparations and to be allowed to take part, at least for the first half-hour, and benefit from being considered adult enough to do so. An understanding guest will not bat an eyelid at being served sticky flapjacks with a bowl of soup!

Try to do things a little differently from when you entertained before—it will help you to begin your new way of life. Try a new recipe or adapt an old one. Look in magazines or the multitude of cookery books that are available which show you how to make a tasty, attractive, but undemanding meal.

KEEPING WELL

A doctor once said that bereavement was like having a surgical operation without an anaesthetic. Certainly you will feel very tired and ache all over, but this is not to say that you must sit down and rest all day. By all means rest whenever you feel a real need to do so, but remember that exercise is also necessary.

A brisk walk each day will give you fresh air and the chance to meet other people for a casual chat. Physical exercise will make you healthily tired so that you sleep better, and will also keep your muscles in trim. Fear and anxiety cause adrenalin to be pumped into the system, making muscles tense.

Adrenalin supplies the energy for bodily activity, so if we don't use our muscles or take enough exercise, it does not get used up. This sets up more tension and frustration.

On the other hand, try not to indulge in a fevered round of activity for its own sake until you are ready to drop with exhaustion. You may find it almost impossible to sit still for any length of time, but one of the most valuable achievements is the ability to relax and clear your mind of anxiety, apprehension and other negative thoughts. To begin with, you may be able to manage only a few minutes, but it will become easier each day and calm you down mentally and physically.

Nurturing the spirit is equally important, so try to keep up friendships, leisure activities, social groups and hobbies, as all these will help to restore a sense of identity and self-worth.

A broken heart

Some people fear they will die of a 'broken heart'. The death of someone close is emotionally shattering, and there may well be an inner feeling of intense pain.

Occasionally, someone who has lost a loved one may suffer some form of heart disease, but it has not been proved that grief alone is the cause. There are nearly always contributory factors. Understandable though it may be for the distressed person to turn to alcohol, drugs or pills to dull the ache, the dangers are well-known and a growing dependence on any of them will not deal with the underlying necessity to work through grief and may cause actual harm.

'I can't sleep'

Most bereaved people say how they dread sleepless nights of tossing and turning, reliving the past and worrying about the future. Commonly the pattern of sleep is so disturbed that the morning brings a headache as bad as the heartache.

Don't worry about not sleeping—that is enough on its own to keep sleep away. Focus instead on what you can do to make things better. There are several options.

First, see your doctor. If they think it necessary, they will prescribe a short course of sleeping pills to break the pattern of sleepless nights.

Being active during the day will encourage natural sleep. A warm bath followed by a warm drink helps you relax. If there is now no one to bring you a drink in bed, take a small vacuum flask of boiling water with you so that you can easily make yourself a drink. Have a tin of biscuits by the bed—you won't sleep if you're hungry.

Make sure you are warm. If you have been used to another person's body warmth in bed, and that person has died, bed can seem exceptionally cold. An electric blanket that is designed to be kept on overnight is one of the most effective sleep inducers ever invented.

Reading and listening

If you like reading in bed, you may find that an undemanding book or a magazine will help switch your mind from its welter of thoughts. Television is another possible diversion. So is a transistor radio. I don't suggest tuning to loud pop music or some stimulating discussion programme, or even a

Ways to help you relax	
◇ Deep, calm breathing	◇ Soothing music
◇ Shoulder shrugs	◇ Warm bath
◇ Rolling head slowly	◇ Light book
◇ Leisurely walk	◇ Radio

phone-in—any of these might send sleep further away than ever! If you are addicted to the news, documentaries, and national and international affairs, you may find the BBC World Service, transmitted right through the night, well worth listening to. The sound of a friendly, and quickly familiar, voice can be a comfort and help soothe you to sleep. Joyce said, 'As soon as I lie down I turn the radio on so that I can hardly hear it. That way I don't really have to listen, even, but it does away with the awful silence of being alone.'

When all else fails, remind yourself that not being able to sleep is not medically harmful. So lie quietly relaxed; make an effort to put from you the worries of the day that has gone and refuse to be anxious about what tomorrow may bring. Try to think of the night as a blessed interlude between one day and the next.

Take advantage of the uninterrupted quiet. This is the time to remember the good things of the past which nothing can take away and to be thankful for what remains.

A sleepless night can be an opportunity to commit yourself into God's loving hands, *expecting* the peace he has promised to all who ask for it. The strength to do all that is demanded of us will come only when it is needed—not before. God's help is always given at the right time.

Of course, this line of thought may mean nothing to you—perhaps you have no links with the Christian church, or have considered yourself 'not religious' for many years. Nevertheless, if you find yourself longing for the comfort of the God who made all things and who is in charge of life and death, then all you need to make a start is to put what I have suggested into your own words.

Eating sensibly

Strong emotion often takes away the desire for food. It is common for the bereaved person to feel full up, even nauseated at the thought of food. Some, even though they feel hungry, will make do with insufficient food because the effort to cook a meal is too great.

But, however little you feel like cooking or eating, it is essential (as when recovering from illness) to get your strength back and live sensibly. It is foolish to risk being a worry to other people, or becoming dependent on them to do something you can do for yourself. Large meals are not called for; it is better to have nutritious foods, little and often.

It makes good sense at any time to keep to a low-fat, low-sugar, high-fibre diet—with plenty of fresh fruit and vegetables which are quick and easy to prepare and may be eaten raw. Be sure to include some protein—meat, fish, cheese and nuts are good protein foods. Drink only moderate amounts of alcohol as it raises the blood pressure. Convenience foods can be good and wholesome (read the ingredients list on the package). Salads with wholemeal bread and cheese makes a tasty, quick meal and a meaty soup with some grated cheese on top is also a meal in itself. Do lay yourself a place at the table or arrange an attractive tray: it makes all the difference.

○ Always have breakfast! It can be just a bowl of cereal and a hot drink, with perhaps a slice of bread or toast. Protein makes it even more nutritious: nuts in the cereal, per-haps, or a boiled egg, or a slice of cheese with the bread.

○ A satisfying, well-balanced lunch could be simply some soup, bread and cheese, a piece of fruit and a drink.

○ If you are hungry in the middle of the afternoon, some carbo-hydrate—bread or a plain cake—and a drink is enough.

○ Supper (preferably cooked) could be meat, beans or pulses, with as many vegetables as you like. Follow it with fruit if you don't want to make a pudding, or yoghurt or ice cream.

Keep up your fluid intake during the day and don't forget a warm drink at bedtime.

Psychological helps

When you are low, it seems impossible to 'think happy'. Yet attitudes of mind *do* influence bodily well-being, so it is a good idea to *expect* something good to happen each day. From there you may be able to plan to make it happen. This is one way towards restoring self-confidence.

Self-respect may be at a low ebb, too, so it is important to keep up your past standards. Tempting though it may be, when you are at home, to slop around the house untidily, it pays to make an effort and dress properly. If you look good it tells those around you that you consider them worth making an effort for.

Even if in the past you have not been concerned about the way you dress, making an effort now can be helpful. Taking the trouble to present yourself well to the outside world is an easy, everyday and practical way to affirm to yourself that you are still important.

Something new to wear, or a record, book or toy, can cheer up a bereaved child.

I am a great believer in what my family calls 'litle treats' for oneself! Many people will have spent all their lives thinking of other people but, especially if you are now living alone, you need to cheer *yourself* up from time to time. This helps to keep at bay the martyr complex. My own brands of self-help are magazines and eating out and, when I have been feeling lower than usual, I have taken myself off to the newsagent and then treated myself to a cup of coffee in the town. Not wildly extravagant indulgences, but such small luxuries can often provide something to look forward to and give a little warmth to bleak days.

THE COMFORT OF FAITH

If you belong to a church, you will find that many people will say, comfortingly, 'Your faith must help you.' But does it?

Christians (or followers of any religion) do not have a monopoly of courage and inner resources. I have been struck time and again by the sheer stoic endurance of people who profess not to believe in God, or in anything other than their own fragile strength. There are countless men and women who, with no religious faith, face bereavement, adjust to it, cope with it and make out of it something good and worthwhile and hopeful.

But faith in God can make a difference. What Christians do have is a trust in the goodness of God: in the hope of life after death, in the confident expectation that he will guide us through life here and now, in the comfort of his presence.

A ninety-year-old lady, married for over sixty years, told me, 'I can only keep going by reminding myself that I still matter to God and that I'm still important to him.'

Bad patches

From time to time, something happens or is said, usually out of the blue, which reopens the old wounds and tears us apart again. One widow told of a morning when the sun was shining, the children were doing well at school and she herself was feeling able to cope with anything. She turned on the radio and heard a voice describing the place where she and her husband had spent their honeymoon. Desolation overcame her and she sat and wept.

Months—even years—after loss, such dark times come and remind us how fragile is our resilience. If we need help, it is only sensible to ask for it. Don't be ashamed of yourself—admit how you feel. An understanding friend or a good neighbour will usually be available to encourage you until the cloud lifts.

People with a religious belief often feel guilty when they are depressed. As a Christian I felt that because faith had upheld me at the time of acute crisis, it would go on doing so automatically. But as time went by, I began to ask questions which had not occurred to me at the beginning, and I felt my faith wavering.

I believe this happens to many Christians. This is when we need to be humble enough to recognize our need of an assurance and encouragement other than our own and to go to someone we can trust, whose opinions we respect. It is possible to rely too much on our own resources of prayer and our own reading of the Bible. It is tempting to read what we want to believe into a section of the Bible or to pray too self-centredly.

Then, a different view may be all we need to set us on our way again. An individual's faith may waver, but God's unfailing love remains faithful to us.

HOW THE CHURCH CAN HELP

Do not hesitate to go into a church at a time of crisis, even if you have never been before or not for many years. Do not hesitate to get in touch with a minister, priest or vicar. One of the church's roles is to be a refuge for those who suffer, and to help any who feel the need to find out if God has something to say to them at a low point in their lives. The church is always there. As a famous archbishop once said, 'The church exists for the people who don't belong to it.' In any church fellowship where Christians are serious about their faith, you will be welcomed and supported, yet not pressured into being 'religious'. That is how God wants Christians to be, and if the first church that you try seems not to offer that kind of support, have the courage to try another.

A fuller life

Many people have found that joining a church where Christians really do aim to live as God wants helps lessen their loneliness. Even in the staidest, stiffest congregations, there is usually someone who is genuinely friendly and ready to help. Some churches have neighbourhood schemes by which they come to hear of people in special need, and many have trained bereavement counsellors. By taking advantage of what the church offers socially, the bereaved can be drawn into activities which they will enjoy and look forward to. After a time some may find they want to attend a service and, against all expectation, discover the beginning of a fuller life, spiritually as well as socially.

Most people will have a church within reach. No one need hesitate to go to the one of their choice; it is perfectly proper to call the minister and ask for help in getting to church, if that is a problem.

In your own time

Nevertheless, for some bereaved Christians, one of the hardest things is to get back into the life of the church. When the whole family once sat, Sunday by Sunday, taking part in the familiar service, going to church may be hard to bear for the person or people left behind. Ruth felt bad because she and the family had not been back since her husband's funeral: 'I just couldn't bear to sing the hymns and the children might cry and I might have had to walk out. It's no use, I can't go.'

But, as always, the sooner we can pick up the threads the easier it will be. However, if the bereaved family feels unable to do this for a time, they should not feel guilty about it. The church shouldn't expect too much too soon. Church members can show the warmth of their caring in practical ways, and by their sympathy and loving comfort. The church is *there*, carrying on its broad shoulders, by its worship and its prayers, all who are in trouble of any kind. Anyone who has experienced this support can fully appreciate the strength which flows from God through the channel of his church.

7
Emotional Problems

LONELINESS

People need people. As the Bible tells us, 'It is not good for man (or woman) to live alone.' The loneliness of bereavement does not consist solely in the loss of the loved one. What is felt equally deeply is the loss of companionship, the sense of belonging, the emotional and often financial security which had existed within the relationship.

People vary in their reaction to loneliness. Some shut themselves off from social contacts, others throw themselves into frenzied attempts to be the life and soul of every gathering. Most of us have pursued a course somewhere between the two. After the death of someone who has been close, we gradually turn to others for company. This is right—it is self-defeating if we become so dependent on having people with us that we can't bear to be alone. We all need some solitude in order to sort ourselves out. It will largely be up to us to arrange our lives so that these times of being alone are balanced by time spent with other people.

Reminders

Just as the setting up of a 'shrine' to the dead person only makes the pain last longer, so it is only common sense to avoid the things you know are likely to upset you—an old photograph, a place which had a special meaning for you both. Some people, though, are comforted by photographs: one man I know had framed every picture of his wife he could find. 'She's in every room of the house,' he said, 'she's still with me.'

But another friend put away everything which would remind her of her dead son. In time, as her anguish lessened, she put up one or two photographs and found they did help her. Do whatever helps ease your loneliness, realizing that life has to go on and that the past must form the future, not restrict it.

Our own life

It can become all too easy to live life through other people—watching television, skipping through magazines, becoming absorbed in the goings on of celebrities or public figures. But it is *our* life we have to live, not someone else's, and it needs to be as full as we can make it. If we want friends in order to relieve our loneliness, we have to be friendly ourselves; to benefit from other people's efforts we have to make efforts ourselves. At first, it will not seem worth it—I remember saying, 'I'm tired of always having to make an effort'—but it is a worthwhile price to pay for our re-entry into the real world and out of the limited one we are in danger of creating around our bruised ego. The worst thing the lonely person can do is sit at home and give in to self-pity.

If you can, go out at least once a day and if possible at about the same time. People are creatures of habit—it will be easier to smile at someone you meet regularly, and soon you will be on speaking terms.

Many new friendships have been formed by such casual encounters. I began to go to a shop in the town for morning coffee. I discovered it had a regular clientele and, after a week or two, people said, 'Hello'. Then it became 'Hello. What awful weather we're having.' Then, 'Hello, are you on your own? May I join you?' Christian names were exchanged and, to this day, I know some of them only by their first names but we consider ourselves friends.

You will have your own style of building friendships. Take courage as you set about the process: some people *are* unfriendly, for all kinds of reasons, but their indifference does not affect your value as a person. Other people will be more welcoming, and every time even a hint of friendship is offered, you can build on that.

A wider horizon

It is surprising but true that there is no need for anyone to be physically alone. Everywhere there are clubs and organizations for the lonely. The bereaved person with a family can become bogged down with child-minding and keeping the home together, so it is important that the horizons should be widened. Joining a group of people with similar interests will do the whole family good. For many people these clubs have provided just what they needed: practical help and moral support. For example, Gingerbread is an organization for single parents and fills a great need of younger parents, relieving their isolation and bringing their children wider contacts.

At the same time, these organizations recognize the dangers of catering for only one type of person—loneliness and separation may be emphasized rather than lessened. And so they all aim at enabling their members gradually to wean themselves away as they feel able.

Information about clubs and organizations can be found in your local library, newspaper or information bureau. The first move is the most difficult but take a deep breath, close your eyes and jump!

SEXUAL AND PHYSICAL LONELINESS

An aspect of bereavement not acknowledged often enough is the physical loneliness. This is frequently the case if the person who has died was the one who offered you physical affection—whether it was a hug, as between parent and child, or an intimate physical relationship, as between partners.

The sense of being physically alone adds to the pain of bereavement. The yearning to be held again can, unfortunately, make relationships that are in reality quite unsuitable seem tempting.

People who have lost their sexual partner may find their

feelings hard to handle. Whatever one may sometimes be told, it is impossible completely to direct one's sexuality into other channels. Death snatches away the deepest human expression of love, leaving an emptiness which nothing else can fill. The sudden cutting-off of the sex life sets up deep tensions.

For most people, of whatever age, the sex drive following bereavement is at a low ebb but as it gradually returns, what to do with it presents a very real problem.

Casual relationships

We all need to hold and be held but to take on some casual sexual relationship is, at best, only a short-term palliative. Without depth and commitment, such an affair is always a second-best substitute. Sympathy runs high for the bereaved and a well-meant offer of 'kindness' can be tempting. The longing to love and be loved is in no way wrong in itself but additional emotional tangles are the last thing we need just now and, for a time at least, we have to get used to being on our own.

For many, masturbation brings temporary and necessary sexual release, but it can never satisfy the basic need to give oneself to another person because there is no mutuality of giving, and the feeling of deprivation may even be intensified.

For anyone who rejects the idea of casual, irresponsible relationships, this is a testing time. Magazines and television all insist that frequent sex is necessary for all, and no concern of anyone except the individuals involved. But Christians believe that the act of sex is the total involvement of one person with another, a complete self-giving. Sex is never an isolated act. There are social as well as personal implications to be considered. Christians believe that sex is a gift from God to be enjoyed but not selfishly exploited. Sexual satisfaction is not to be an irresponsible indulgence.

Those who have not actually lost a sexual relationship also need to be wary. In their craving simply to be held close, they might find themselves setting up relationships with a sexual aspect that will only lead to hurt. Indeed, many people find themselves becoming emotionally attached to their counsellors and longing for a deeper relationship with them. Professionals in this area are well aware of this risk, and their codes of conduct insist that they avoid any kind of physical contact that could be misinterpreted. It is worth setting the same code of conduct for yourself.

This does not mean that you have to cut yourself off. At a time when I was experiencing intense physical loneliness, I read some perceptive words by a young American widow: 'While the human organism can get along without physical love-making, it cannot thrive without human affection.' What the bereaved need most is warm concern and continuing love and tenderness. Over and over again we realize that the greatest blessings of all are thoughtful families and faithful friends. The Christian image of the church being a family of brothers and sisters who truly love each other gives an idea of the kind of relationship that can be most helpful at this time.

BUILDING NEW RELATIONSHIPS

At the time of bereavement, the idea of somehow replacing the family relationship that has been lost will be unthinkable. However, new relationships will be formed.

Those who have been widowed may insist that they will never remarry. In fact, a high proportion of widowers do so within five years of losing their wives. The figure for widows is much lower. In his bereavement studies, Murray Parkes has noted that many widows still seem to regard themselves as married to their dead husbands and remarriage represents for them a form of infidelity. Widows are often afraid that children will resent any male who seems to them to be usurping the place of their dead father. Widowers believe that children have deep-seated difficulties in accepting a stepmother. Bereaved parents with several young children feel that no one will be willing to take on a whole new family.

It may appear that those who 'remain faithful' to a dead spouse are particularly noble but a second marriage should be seen as a compliment to the previous partner. If your marriage was a good and fulfilling one, built on mutual and unselfish love, you will feel able to undertake a second commitment believing that this is what your husband or wife would have wanted for you. Never think of it as being in any way disloyal. Every relationship is unique. No one need condemn themselves to a bleak lifetime of living on past memories and loyalties.

There is often a deep fear of entering into a new commitment with the possibility of having to bear the same loss again. Conversely, a dread of being alone can lead to impulsive or wrong decisions being made. In this area, particularly, such decisions should be deferred until a measure of emotional stability has been recovered.

Even so, many do feel a sense of betrayal when contemplating a second marriage. Before entering into a new relationship it is essential to say goodbye to the old one—not forgetting it, but letting it go, never allowing it to come between you and your new life.

A second marriage calls for courage, commitment and a degree of tolerance which can be demanding. It is essential to give each other space, to respect the need at times to be alone or to do things separately. But, given the essential ingredients of love and understanding, making it work can bring a deep sense of achievement and fulfilment.

There are other family relationships that can be established, too. Of course, the person who has died cannot be replaced, but your ability to make a relationship—as a parent, as a child, as a cousin—can be used again, as you welcome new friends into the circle of your life. Both you and the other person can derive a great deal of joy from such a relationship.

Realistic expectations

Bereavement weakens one's self-confidence and the longing for support is sometimes overwhelming, especially when

71

there are awesome tasks to be faced, such as running a business or bringing up young children or, especially for older people, simply having to handle everyday affairs previously undertaken by husband or wife. The prospect of having someone to share the responsibility can be very attractive.

Much of the tension which may arise early in a second marriage comes from fear that you may not live up to the expectations of your new spouse, or that you may not compare favourably with the first wife or husband. But you are both as you are *now*, and a second marriage should be seen as a new beginning to both your lives. If a first marriage was happy, a second is likely to be so, too. Past experience will have shown that allowances have to be made on both sides, respect shown for each other's emotional privacy, and any wisdom you gained from your first partnership brought to bear on the second.

Other relationships, such as that of 'adoptive' grandparents or grandchildren, are usually informal, and so there is less pressure on them. However, it is important to bear in mind that your hopes for the relationship may be far greater than those of the other person: you may want to be as close as family; they may regard you as one of several friends. Be glad for what each relationship can offer, rather than being disappointed at what is lacking.

Step-parents and step-children

If your new relationship provides a step-parent for your children, you will have special challenges. By the time of your marriage, the children will usually already have come to know their new step-parent well. Hopefully, they will be happy for you. However, it may be, especially if they are still very young, that they will guard your love for them jealously, not wanting to share you with anyone else. In this situation, you will need to reassure them that you still love them just as much. You have to point out that love is not limited, and do so in a way they can understand. Love generates love and this new relationship, while in no way

72

being a replacement of a loved parent can, with their co-operation, help the whole family back to happiness.

SHARING YOUR HOME

If the prospect of living alone is unbearable, you may consider setting up house with a friend or relative. This arrangement can be highly successful—it can also be quite disastrous. The saying, 'You never really know a person until you live with them' is very true. Ensure that you will be able to get on together before committing yourself. Take time to talk about your interests, families, likes and dislikes. Bear in mind that you may both find it difficult to adapt.

When you have decided on a person you think suitable, it may help if you agree that the first fortnight will be a trial period, if circumstances make this possible. At the end of that time, you'll know how you get along together.

When you are thinking of any kind of sharing, it is wise to have a proper agreement drawn up so that each person knows exactly what is expected. Fix a fair rent for the area if appropriate; and agree a method of splitting gas, electricity and phone bills and household expenses. This sounds cold-blooded, but it will save much argument if difficulties should arise later on.

Fair deal

A shared home usually means that one of you will have to give up most of your own furniture and goods, and may always feel hard done by. Discuss this honestly beforehand. Certain questions will have to be asked:

◇ How are the financial arrangements to work?

◇ Will you live separate lives or do most things together?

◇ Having decided what you want, can you see the other person being willing to co-operate on those terms?

◇ How far are *you* willing to give way?

8
The Bereaved Child

What do you say when a child announces the news that a friend's mummy or daddy has died? Most people's immediate reaction is to say 'How dreadful!' and change the subject. But the child may be frightened and bewildered, hit by the fact that death happens not only on television but to real people and therefore, perhaps, even their own parents.

Talking about death

This is when we should stop whatever we are doing, express our own shock and sorrow and speak naturally about what has happened. Ask the child if there is anything you could do to help. Suggest being particularly kind to the friend—asking them round to play, for example.

This way of dealing with a terrifying situation will do much to reassure. It gives children a chance to help their friend practically. Thinking of things *they* might be able to do will reduce their feelings of helplessness. It will also give them a sense of security to learn that even a disaster like this can be coped with.

WHEN DEATH COMES

We must never try to shut children out of the grief the whole family shares. It is impossible, as well as undesirable, completely to protect them from what has happened, and they will be more likely to suffer permanent emotional damage if they feel excluded and left to face their fears and anxieties by themselves. This is particularly the case when the subject of death has always been swept under the carpet or glossed over.

The most unobtrusive way of allowing children to be

aware of death is by helping them to see that, from time to time, suffering of some sort comes into every life and that death is the inevitable and natural end of life. They will recognize this fact when the cat brings in a bird or a mouse it has killed. They will have seen it in nature programmes on TV.

Many will experience it for the first time in the death of a dearly-loved pet, and here it is important to discover what will most help the child. In one family I knew, when the old and ailing budgie died, the three children arranged a funeral service for it before burying it at the bottom of the garden. The parents wisely made no comment, were solemnly invited to the ceremony, and felt afterwards that it had been a valuable experience for the whole family.

A form of bereavement which many children suffer is when a best friend moves away. For a child, this sort of separation is a little death and can be quite desperate. However the suffering comes, our part is to reassure children that they are not alone in their sadness, that they can cry or tell us how they are feeling because among ourselves and within the family we all share our sorrows.

Never tell lies

On the death of a parent, one child was told that her daddy had gone abroad, another that her mummy was in hospital. Both children eventually learned the truth and then suffered a shock made worse by the permanent distrust they came to feel for all adults and the fear that any separation might mean death. Interestingly, when they themselves became parents, their own children were thought to be particularly clinging.

Within a Christian family, honesty has to extend even further. The child who said bitterly that God was 'no good' was reacting perfectly rationally to his father's death in a plane crash, for his mother had often said that God would keep him safe. Children should learn, but gently, that Christians are not immune to disaster and human tragedy. The assurance is that, for those whose lives are committed to God, whatever happens cannot ultimately destroy either the person who has died or those left behind. God holds us in his love and knows what to do (always so important to a child) so that, in the end, everything will be all right (equally important). The sorrow which has come to us should give us a greater understanding of and sympathy for all who suffer. If you believe that death is not the end, helpful analogies can be drawn—the butterfly emerging from the chrysalis is one often used.

Some common fears

On top of the shock of unbelief at the death of a parent is the frequent fear of losing the other as well. Children may ask the surviving parent, 'How old are you? Are *you* going to die?' Young children may even think that everyone else in the family is about to die.

Imaginative children may be frightened that the parent's ghost will return and haunt them. Bedtime is dreaded and brings on symptoms such as sweating, bed-wetting and nightmares. 'Can Daddy see me?' Some children insist on having the window closed 'in case Daddy comes in'.

Younger children may worry that their mummy or daddy will marry someone else, especially if they have read old-fashioned stories about wicked step-mothers. In such cases, the parent must explain that friends who drop by to offer help are simply that, and not future step-parents.

It is important to allow children to talk about their fears, so that the hidden ones can be brought into the open and dealt with. Encourage them to talk about the dead parent. If they are not able to show their feelings, seeing and hearing other members of the family openly expressing their own and exchanging their memories may help them to loosen up. If children withdraw into themselves, we have to watch their reactions carefully. We must be sensitive in trying to understand what may be making them anxious or too shocked to confide in us.

A constructive attitude

Children's attitude to death will be coloured by what they

have learned from the grown-ups who care for them. If they have been taught compassion for others, they will find it easier to accept bereavement. They have been taught to help their friends; now they will tend to assume it is the turn of those friends to help them! This expectation will provide reassurance and reduce any sense of isolation.

Fear, guilt and shock

The effects of bereavement on children depends on many things: age, personality and the reactions of the family. When a parent dies, the children feel deserted and abandoned. Was it because they were naughty or disobedient? Guilt and self-doubt build up. They remember the time they said, 'I wish you were dead', and may believe they have actually killed mummy or daddy. John cried bitterly when his brother died: 'I said "Drop dead" to him last week when we were playing.'

Older children can appear almost nonchalant in the face of death. When Susan came home from school, she was told that her mother had been killed in a car crash. 'Has she?' she said, 'is tea ready?' This type of reaction is due to intense shock and is an automatic defence mechanism against believing the unbelievable, so it would be out of place to accuse her of callousness.

On the other hand, an older child may revert to baby ways or else assume an unnaturally adult attitude. In some ways adolescents are even more vulnerable than younger children and may feel unable to bear the grief of the parent as well as their own. They may then withdraw from the family, sharing their feelings only with close peer-group friends; but, whatever their reactions, we must never assume that grief is not present.

Again, a parent may not be the best person to deal with the anxiety, anger or depression which threatens to overwhelm the young person; a minister, a youth leader, teacher, family friend or godparent can prove invaluable. All that matters is that it is someone the young person is comfortable with and whose judgment they trust.

How much to tell children about death should always depend on how much they want to know. This will be discovered by the sort of questions they ask.

Children realize that death marks the end of life (though, as Christians believe, the beginning of another) and that death brings sorrow and grief. But children are as resilient as they are vulnerable, and with help and support they can survive almost any experience, as long as they are surrounded by love.

The way in which we describe death will depend on our own beliefs, but we have to remember that children are matter-of-fact thinkers. Children tend to believe the dead person is in another place. 'Where is he? Will he have breakfast there?' We shall dig a pit of our own making if we use such expressions as 'gone to sleep'— 'When will he wake up?'; 'gone to heaven'—'Why? How long for?'; 'passed away'—'What do you mean?' The phrase 'gone to sleep' can also provoke night-time fears that the same thing may happen to them. Such euphemisms do nothing to soften the blow and may cause deeper confusion. Children may realize already that dead things are buried or burned; if so, they will more easily be able to accept that this is what happens to dead people as well. This is a stark fact but, in the end, facts explained with loving calmness are more reassuring than false hopes.

Answering their questions

When something touches them deeply and personally, the questions children ask are among the most difficult for the adult to answer. Although death at a ripe old age may be straightforward to explain, none of us knows why death comes to someone young and healthy. Nor do we actually *know* what happens after death has taken place.

All questions have to be treated seriously. We have to be as honest as possible according to our own beliefs. These may not be completely understood by children at the time but will give a framework on which they can build as time goes by.

I firmly believe that a background of Christian belief does much to comfort children at this time. We are able to assure them that, although we don't know why death has come to mummy or daddy or to some other member of the family, we do know that the love of God is unshakeable and holds us all, in life and in death, and that nothing can separate us from God or the one who has died.

This, of course, is far too abstract for a grieving child fully to take in, but in our own case I found that it was possible to illustrate this by pointing out that all the kindness, invitations, flowers and letters that we received were God's way of showing us his love by sending other people to look after us. 'Who do you think will ask us out on Saturday?' became a regular mid-week question!

CHILDREN'S MOURNING

To mourn is just as much a psychological necessity for children as it is for adults and it cannot be rushed. They need time to be sad, to remember, to work through the feelings of bewilderment and loss. It may help them if they talk about their feelings so that they come to understand what is going on inside them, and so can cope with their emotional conflict.

Very young children will not be able to identify different aspects of their grief; they will simply feel a diffused sense of sadness and anxiety. Time has little meaning and so assurances about next week or next year will mean nothing. As with a deeply grieving adult, they need to be cuddled and held close.

The child and parent both need the same patient, loving care. They will also need times to be by themselves quietly if they are to come to terms with what has happened and find a degree of acceptance drawing on their own resources. No one can do this for them.

Eight-year-old Neil, wise beyond his years, used to announce, 'I am going upstairs to do my thinks.'

Going to the funeral

It is natural to wish to spare children the ordeal of the

funeral service, but we should think again. Children may well feel they are not wanted and are being excluded from some important and mysterious occasion. It is unlikely that they will have been to a funeral before; they will have little idea of what it is all about, and their imaginations may paint terrifying pictures. Adults may be too bound up in their own grief to guess what is going on in a child's mind.

Some children have thought that people have to go and look at the dead person. One child thought that all the doctors would be there to try and make the body come alive again. A five-year-old girl who was going to be looked after by a neighbour refused to stay in the house in case the dead person 'got away' and ran back home.

If the child is given a simple explanation beforehand of what will happen at the funeral and is then allowed to be present, many such fears will be exorcized. It also helps the child, like the adult, to face the reality of death. However harrowing the sight of a grieving or distraught child may be to other people, children need to face the truth so that the healing process can begin. Attending the funeral can be of positive help provided someone is there to answer all their questions and to be sensitive to their needs, to tell as much as they ask and to hear what has been left unasked and so avoid the invention of upsetting fantasies.

Patterns of behaviour

Many children react to death with anti-social behaviour and aggressiveness, disguising their fear by demanding that everything should be all right again. Bereaved children may be hostile to other members of the family; they may be rude or unnaturally noisy.

Generally speaking, children under the age of five appear to ignore the fact of death because it is beyond their understanding, though they will be well aware of the atmosphere of distress in the home and will respond with various anxiety symptoms, often becoming demanding and clinging.

Between the ages of five and nine, they may think of

death as a punishment on them for their naughtiness and that, if they are 'good', the dead person will come back again. This is why it is important for this age group to attend the funeral and be helped to realize death's finality.

It is not until they are ten or eleven that children understand death more fully.

Following the first shock and tears, there often follows a period of quiet despair. Children may become withdrawn and unable to concentrate on anything. As a result, school work will suffer. They may become weepy, wet the bed, give in to tempers and tantrums. They need reassurance that this is perfectly normal and is nature's way of providing a rest until they are strong enough to take the strain. We have to judge when the time has come to nudge them out of themselves once more.

If all or any such symptoms persist or worsen, a doctor's advice should be sought. Dealing with young children whose behaviour patterns have become unpredictable and demanding is very hard for the bereaved parent. Just when they need all their own emotional strength and resources, they are called upon by their children for support and comfort. Little wonder that they sometimes find it too much to cope with. This is where neighbours, friends, the church and the school can all provide a practical helping hand which can prevent the situation getting out of control.

Helping the child recover

By talking to the children and giving them plenty of time to talk to us, we help each other. In times of grief, habit is a great help. Children should go to school as usual and be encouraged to do jobs about the house. This will give them a renewed sense of purpose. Their self-esteem can be raised by asking them what they think would most help other members of the family. Children often see their brothers and sisters more clearly than the parent does and come up with imaginative suggestions which we would never have thought of. 'Do you know, Mummy,' said Jane, the youngest of the family, 'I think Peter (five years older) would like to colour my new picture book. We could pretend *I* want him to do it.'

Schools can play a vital part. There will almost certainly be several other children at school whose mother, father or sibling has died, along with many whose grandparents have died. Although insensitive and cruel in other ways, children treat a bereaved friend much more kindly and naturally than the adult world treats the bereaved parent, with less of the embarrassment or awkwardness felt by the grown-ups. In my experience, teachers, too, go out of their way to support the child, and should always be told what has happened, especially if exams are looming, and kept in the picture as to how *you* think the child is managing.

The extended family can be of great value to a bereaved child at this time. Grandparents can do so much to help, giving them time, listening, empathizing and encouraging. They, too, will be mourning someone they loved so they and the child can grieve together. In addition, their age and experience should be able to bring a wider perspective to the situation so that the reassurance they can offer will carry a certain authority which the child can recognize and accept.

Uncles and aunts have a part to play as well. An older girl will welcome a trip with a sympathetic and generous aunt and the opportunity to talk to another woman not quite so closely affected by what has happened. For older boys, some sort of male role model is essential and an uncle can help fill this gap in several practical ways by getting involved with their interests and activities, discussing 'masculine' subjects in a man-to-man way.

The impact of a grandparent's death on a child should not be underestimated, and it is important for them to have someone to turn to when their parents are grieving too.

Anything which raises self-esteem and self-confidence will ease the sense of rejection or insignificance. The bereaved *child* needs to be given attention as well as the parent. (See also the chapter *How Others Can Help*—Help from the family.)

Outside help

Although the family should not shut itself away, we should be wary about accepting invitations on the children's behalf too soon after the death. Balance is essential at first, and some people are tempted to stay indoors in miserable isolation. Many teenagers, however, will feel that their entire social life has been cut off. They may be protective of the parent's feelings: 'Will you mind if I go to the club on Saturday and would it be all right to wear my red shirt?' 'Tony's asked me to a gig next Tuesday. Can I go? I haven't been out since Mum died. I don't know what's been happening.'

With younger children it can be counter-productive to push them out against their will. We must decide carefully whether they need protecting a little longer or whether they should be given a gentle push. One solution is to encourage their friends into your home. This will also be good for you if it is your partner who has died; it will now be more necessary than ever to keep up with youthful attitudes and ideas as you embark on bringing up a family single-handed. On a practical level, it will also be a means of meeting their parents and making new friends.

9

The One-Parent Family

ADAPTATION

Bringing up children single-handed is hard work and there is no virtue in trying to be independent and going it alone. Other people are willing to lend a hand, and all offers of help should be accepted. Neighbours and friends will sometimes offer to take children to a show or a concert or a day trip or even on holiday with their own families. They are often very willing to act as surrogate mothers or fathers, and can be particularly helpful in taking an interest in 'typically male' or 'typically female' activities that children used to enjoy with the the parent who has died. It does the grieving members of a family good to get away from each other for a time, and it is shortsighted to refuse such kindnesses. Anything which will widen the horizons and lead to renewed interest in the 'normal' world is to be welcomed.

Parents' roles

It very quickly becomes obvious that it is impossible for anyone to be both mother and father. Losing a parent means that the family is incomplete and all its members have to learn to live within the new limitations. In our own case, I tried to take an intelligent interest in my sons' current passions. I watched televized sport with them and found I was becoming hooked. Football was similar to hockey, I decided—but to this day the finer rules of rugby escape me. I spent long hours sitting on remote railway station platforms waiting for the one train of the day to rumble past so that times and numbers could be checked and entered in little red books. For their part, the boys even tolerated sessions of Wimbledon and became more partisan than the most dedicated schoolgirls.

Children have an innate sense of fair play and the boys co-operated by entering into some of my hobbies, offering advice on knitting patterns and designs, suggesting ideas for talks/broadcasts/articles—and always ready to try out extraordinary recipes for meals!

Where to go for help

Not every single-parent family is surrounded by good friends and neighbours. Not all bereaved adults are able to cope. The parent often feels isolated and alone with their problems, but several organizations exist to give advice and practical help. (See list of organizations given in the chapter *What will it mean?*)

LOOKING FORWARD

As the time comes for future plans to be made, the parent can do much to restore drooping self-confidence by involving the children. It is frightening for them to think that decisions are being made which will affect them deeply but in which they have no say.

When it became obvious that we would have to move, we all went, as a family, to look at houses. The children's priorities were not exactly the same as mine. They were more interested in whether the garden would be big enough for a football pitch! But, to my surprise, they were able to make sensible and practical observations, some of which I hadn't been aware of. When we did find a house, we felt it had been a joint decision and one we had all agreed on.

But as they grow up, children may turn to others outside the family to discuss some problem they would rather not talk about to their parent. As parents, we must not resent this; our main concern is that they grow up wisely, no matter who helps them do so. Our task is to supply the security they need to enter into the full life which is their birthright. There must never be pressure on a child to stay at home to keep mother or father company. We bring up children solely to equip them to leave us, free and independent.

Remarriage

Freedom is also our right—we may remarry, and if we have taught our children respect for individual freedom, they will understand. Provided that we and our children have 'let go' of the dead parent, this new relationship can be welcomed and entered into with hope. Reassure the children that to remarry is not disloyal to the previous partner, nor does it mean that they have been forgotten. (See also the chapter *Emotional Problems*, Remarriage —step-children.)

Closer family life

Any study of one-parent families is bound to look depressing. But most families do survive—not unmarked, but with scars that heal. Families with a forward-looking approach and a faith or philosophy to carry them along have the best chance.

As the ranks close, bereavement can result in a closer family intimacy. Discipline can be simpler when there is only one parent to draw up the rules and, in the new atmosphere of mutual concern, you can explain why certain things are not allowed. Children will sometimes read the riot act to a sibling and justify it with 'Think of Mum/Dad.'

The dreaded generation gap can also be bridged; grief is a great leveller and when you have all seen each other with the defences down and deepest feelings expressed, such controversial subjects as sex, politics, money and religion become easier to discuss.

Of course, it will never be all sweetness and light. Some families tear themselves apart with bitter mutual recriminations; some single parents will take it out on the children; some children will be belligerent, aggressive or totally unco-operative. In such potentially destructive circumstances, it is sensible to call on outside help and advice.

New achievements

In a newspaper article, a lone father put his own hopeful views. He said, 'The one-parent family only survives if it pulls together. I used to tell my daughters, "Put into it as much as you take out."' He got to know his children thoroughly and felt a great sense of achievement in attending to their individual needs and emotions. It gave an unexpected extra dimension to his life and he thinks that his daughters have been able to carry this attitude over into their marriages.

10

Where to Live—and How

The roof over our head and the housekeeping budget are things we like to be able to take for granted. When a family member dies, you may find that these no longer seem secure. Fortunately, most questions can be left for a while until you are better able to deal with them.

Decisions, decisions

The golden rule is not to do anything in a hurry. If it is at all possible, major decisions about lifestyle should be postponed for at least six months and preferably for a year. At first, your judgment is unlikely to be reliable and it will be difficult to see things clearly. A line of action which seemed right at the time may later prove to have been a mistake.

Never be afraid to ask for advice and opinion on these matters. Most people are more than willing to make suggestions. Not all of these will be equally helpful, but accept them in the spirit in which they are given, weigh up all the arguments and keep them in your mind until you feel able to come to a sensible decision. It is a good idea to write suggestions down as memory is unreliable.

Good neighbours will help out in a household emergency. The local priest or minister will want to share with you Christian comfort and strength at a time of bereavement, and provide practical support.

HOW SHALL WE MANAGE?

The death of a close family member can have a devastating impact on finances. In situations where this is the case, the first problem to solve is how to manage with the money available.

It may be that the person who has died took charge of running the home and caring for the family members: the mother of a small family, perhaps, or the grown-up son who did all the maintenance. Now, it may be necessary to pay someone to do that work, or reorganize the time you spend in paid employment in order to do that work yourself.

If you have to find someone to provide virtually full-time help—a nanny for young children, perhaps, or a nurse for an invalid—that can be extremely expensive. Friends and relatives may be able to provide help in the short-term, but it is rare for them to be able to take on such a big commitment for a longer period.

A basic year's budget

As soon as you know how much money will be available for living expenses, it helps to draw up a simple budget, at least for the first year. You may prefer to think in months rather than years, but it is the whole year's expenses that matter. These can add up to an alarming amount, and a detailed list of what they are and when they are due will make it easier to see where cutbacks have to be made.

If you have not been used to keeping accounts, the idea of writing down everything you spend, even day-to-day shopping, may seem a real chore. But it soon becomes routine and provides a quick check whenever you need to see where you have under- or over-spent. It also makes you feel incredibly efficient!

Once your financial position is clear, it is worth asking the social security department whether you are eligible for any extra allowances.

Making economies

Once you have budgeted for essentials like your mortgage and statutory outgoings, you can then see where it may be possible to economize. It is important not to cut down on items such as proper food, but it is often relatively simple to save quite large amounts by reorganizing your largest expenses.

If you own a car, you may be able to manage without—or least with a smaller one.

Heaters can be adjusted so that rooms are kept at slightly lower temperatures which you will hardly notice, and switched off altogether in rooms not being used. Efficient loft insulation and the lagging of hot-water pipes and the tank will also cut fuel costs, as will double glazing—if you can afford it!

Shopping becomes more economical if you make a list of what you *need* and stick to it, rather than wandering round the shelves when you may pick up items which are not strictly necessary.

Good quality—even trendy—clothes can be bought in the charity shops which abound in every high street.

Holidays out of the peak season or bargain breaks cut costs in that area.

As well as finding ways to cut costs, people who do have the support of a wider community, such as a church, may find all kinds of ways to share expenses: someone with a car may offer shopping trips to town on a regular basis; there may be a swap-shop for clothes that still have lots of life in them; groups of people may share expensive equipment, such as lawn-mowers; others may barter their skills in hairdressing, car maintenance and so on. This kind of sharing may even provide some luxuries—perhaps a holiday cottage or caravan that someone is more than willing to rent out to people they know at affordable prices.

When you have worked out your income and expenditure and decided where you can reasonably cut back, have another look to see if it will be possible to allocate a sum, however small, for little luxuries and extras to treat yourself and the family to from time to time so that life does not become more careful than it need.

WHERE SHALL WE LIVE?

There are three common reactions to bereavement. One is a feeling that you must stay where you are: 'I can never leave this house; I feel he/she is still here with me.' Another is an urge to move right away to a new area where no one knows you and where you can start again. More common still is the desire to move in order to be near a relative or friend.

Be careful

A decision to move house should only be taken after careful thought. All too often one hears of a hurried move to another part of the country where the bereaved person no longer has the comfort of familiar landmarks and lifestyle, finds that few people are interested in their troubles, and has great difficulty in making new friends.

One elderly widower could not bear to go on living in the old home after his wife died, so against all advice he sold up and bought a house in the same town as his married daughter. Soon after, his son-in-law was sent abroad for two years and the old man had no one of his own to visit or talk

---

Household Management Budget

Expenditure

◇ Food and drink

◇ Telephone and postage

◇ Electricity, gas and coal

◇ Insurance

◇ Mortgage, council tax and rent

◇ Hire purchase/credit card commitments

◇ House repairs, renewals and maintenance

◇ Gifts, subscriptions and donations

◇ Clothes

◇ Savings

◇ Emergencies

Leisure

◇ Car and travel

◇ Holidays

◇ Entertainments and hobbies

Income

◇ Earnings

◇ Investments

◇ Pensions

◇ Allowances

to. He became more and more of a recluse, and before the two years were up, he too had died.

There are now several thousand housing associations—independent organizations which aim to provide good rented accommodation. Find out about schemes in your area.

If you find it difficult to pay your rent you may be able to claim a rent rebate. The amount depends on your total income, your rent, and your family circumstances. Apply at the rent rebates section at your local council offices. *There's money off rent*, from your local council offices or Citizens' Advice Bureau, gives further information.

Of course, it can be a good idea to move. The important thing to remember is that this step should only be taken when you are sure you are no longer dependent on your present neighbours and environment. For parents, the decision to move will probably be made when the last child leaves home. For others, the decision may come when friends retire and move away. By then, you will be able to see more clearly what you want to do and where you want to be.

When a couple have been sharing a home, the surviving partner may have no choice but to give up their home; lack of money forces it on them and they have to look around for a smaller house which will be cheaper to run. Some will be able to stay where they are, however, either because their partner's life insurance was linked to the mortgage or because they have a sufficiently high income. In that case, see your solicitor to make sure the deeds of the house are adjusted to your name only.

Restlessness

Acute restlessness is common in bereavement. This may take the form of frequent visits to people around the country. Friends and relatives will not like to say no when you invite yourself for a day or two, but hectic travel is best avoided or at least postponed. Other people lead busy lives and may be nervous that they will not be able to offer the support you may need.

The wife of someone I knew was widowed while she and her husband were on holiday. The chain of events following her bereavement presents a classic example of bad advice. She sold the house from a distance because she could not bear the thought of coming back; she moved round the country from married child to married child; she stayed two or three nights with various friends in turn, living out of her suitcase for months on end.

She never came to terms with what had happened, was bereft of old friends in her own neighbourhood, at the mercy of estate agents and quack medical opinions, and prey to every fear that a vivid imagination could produce. In the end she bought a cottage in a remote Northumberland village where she and her husband had once spent a holiday, and she gradually became more and more depressed and apathetic.

You can't run away from your situation. Wherever you go, your grief goes with you, dissolving only slowly and undramatically, like the thaw after a long winter. Until you have worked through it, you are better in your own place, among people you know well. Gradually, you will begin to feel a sense of purpose and the possibility of returning happiness. *Then* is the time to plan for the future.

Staying where you are

In the same way, it isn't always a good idea to accept kindly-meant offers of hospitality immediately after bereavement. Going away is always easier than coming back. If you feel you must have extra support—either because there will be no one else in the house or because there are young children to cope with—accept an offer from someone sympathetic to come and stay with you for a short time. That way, you will not sit about with nothing to do but think, you will not have to be a 'good guest', and you will be able to do the day-to-day jobs as usual.

Sometimes, to be in someone else's house, with little to do and too much time in which to worry about what needs to be done at home, adds to the alarm and frustration. It is better to stick it out and begin to come to terms with the situation, and then, when you feel reasonably confident of being able to return home without too much pain, to spend a short time away with friendly and agreeable people.

By that time you will be needing a rest and will be able to relax better for knowing that immediate decisions have been taken and jobs attended to. Being away from it all will then provide a sense of balance and proportion to enable you to look ahead sensibly. When you do go back, it helps immeasurably to have someone with you just long enough to see you settled in.

If you have to move

It is doubly hard that the problems of finding a new home come at a time when you are least able to cope with it all.

There may be a long waiting-list for council property. Even if you have been renting from a local authority, you may find the tenancy is not transferable. If you move away from the district and apply to the new authority, you will of course go to the bottom of the list and have to find temporary accommodation.

If you are over fifty-five, it is well worth considering sheltered housing. In most areas there is such accommodation, although there may be a waiting list for those owned by local councils. If you own your own property, you might consider selling and buying into private sheltered accommodation. These flats or bungalows are usually built to a high standard of comfort. Whether council or privately owned, such accommodation provides independence but with the back-up of a warden in case of emergencies, a community life if you wish, or total privacy behind your own front door.

Kathleen's life was transformed when she moved into her sheltered flat. Since becoming a widow, she had been living in a too-large house, she could no longer cope with the garden and she was deteriorating in isolation and apathy. Within a month of her move, she had asked one or two of the other residents in for tea, organized a weekly get-together in the communal lounge, accepted the post of treasurer for the Christmas club, and was wondering about starting a bridge club. She became more truly alive in six months than she had been for the previous six years. 'And,' she said, 'I'm not a worry to my family any more.'

Living with relatives

Again, be careful! However tempted and pressurized you may be, think hard before agreeing to live with relatives. The practical objection to this is that once you have found a roof over your head, the local authority may well assume that there is no hurry to rehouse you and may even move your name lower down the list. If you have sold your own house, you will have burned your boats almost irrevocably—will you ever feel like embarking on a search for another if it doesn't work out?

You may also have had to sell most of your possessions and will have to get used to living in someone else's surroundings. You may come to feel more of a lodger than a sharer and a creeping resentment may develop. Understanding and adaptable though your relatives may be, everyone needs somewhere of their own where they can work out their problems and attitudes independently, free from criticism or unwanted advice.

Of course, there are many cases where such a solution has proved successful and rewarding for all concerned—it's just that such a step should not be rushed.

11
Earning a Living

PROS AND CONS

After where to live, the most pressing problem will be how to make enough money to live on. This will be particularly hard in cases where bereavement means that a major income is lost. It can be just as hard if the work that used to be done by the person who has died now has to be paid for.

For some people, the best option may be to change the type of work they do: get a paid job, perhaps, or a second job—or take a job with lower pay but a more flexible work schedule. There are pros and cons to be considered.

○ Will the money you earn reduce the benefits to which you are entitled?

○ Will money be stopped if you are off sick?

○ Will going out to work mean that you have to pay out more—for domestic help, perhaps?

○ Will your earnings push up your tax liability?

○ Will a less pressured job give you the satisfaction and the money that you need?

MAKING YOUR HOUSE WORK FOR YOU

If you own your house but may have difficulty in keeping it going, how can the house itself help? Have you, or can you improvise, a spare room? If so, would you be willing to let it? Universities and colleges are always desperate to find accommodation for both staff and students, and if you live near one you are likely to find plenty of takers.

However, letting a room or rooms is not always

advantageous. It may cost you more in light, heat and upkeep than it will bring in. Check, also, that any housing benefit will be unaffected, and whether there are any tax considerations to take into account.

Do remember, also, that you may not get on with your lodger. They may have very different sleeping times to you, and different ideas about noise level! Don't rush into finding someone.

Finding a lodger

The advantage of letting a room to someone connected with education is that you will probably have the holidays free, while still receiving a small retaining fee. Decide whether you would prefer to give someone full board, bed, breakfast and evening meal, bed and breakfast, or accommodation only. Find out whether your lodger will be there at weekends and if so whether the same meal arrangements will apply. If you have a job outside the home, will you be able to provide meals or will it be better for you to be independent of each other in this respect? Discuss with them whether they wish to share everything with you and your family, or whether they are to live on a bed-sit basis, with shared bathroom, cooking in their room.

Decide whether you want a man, woman, boy or girl. What sort of age would you prefer—a young student, a slightly older person, a middle-aged person perhaps on a temporary assignment in your area? Another adult or near-adult in the house has definite advantages: it means that someone else will be there in case of household disasters or sudden illness; they can also provide new ideas, a more balanced view of life. The mere fact of someone coming in and out may give that extra sense of security you need. A lodger with whom you get on well can be a help in many ways, and be someone else in the house if you are living alone.

The legal side

You should certainly seek legal advice on drawing up a

proper tenancy agreement to protect you from undesirable
tenants. In the UK, once your tenant has signed the tenancy
agreement, you are bound by law to give them a rent book
(these can be bought from most stationers). Every time you
receive the rent, your tenant should produce the book and
you sign it as a receipt. Even if the tenant is someone you
know, it is in both your interests to place everything on a
formal and legal footing.

If you live in rented accommodation, and want to sub-let
a room, you will need to ask your landlord for written
permission. (A local authority, unfortunately, often puts
your rent up when you let a room.) If you have a mortgage,
you will likewise need to obtain permission to let from your
building society.

When you make your tax return you must include any
rent you have received. You can, however, deduct the cost
of such expenses as preparing the room, putting right any
damage caused, and necessary replacement of furnishings.

Home Income schemes

These are arrangements similar in some ways to a mortgage.
In the UK this service is often provided by insurance
companies. You agree a sum of money which they will pay
you as a regular income in return for holding your house as
security. At your death, the money they have paid you will
be deducted from your estate. It is well worth looking into
such schemes, especially if you are unable or too old to
obtain employment and money is a bit tight. But professional explanation and advice should be sought before you
enter into any agreement.

WORKING OUTSIDE THE HOME

Evaluating your job

If you have been in paid employment up to the time of
bereavement, the question of working outside the home
may be quite straightforward. The best option may simply
be to continue in your work. If you have been with your

employer for a reasonable period, and given good service, you are likely to find that they will be reasonably sympathetic to your situation, and allow some flexibility in your working arrangement for a little time afterwards. This can be an immense benefit.

In the longer term, however, you may decide that the job no longer suits you as well as before. Perhaps you need more free time, more regular hours, or less travelling that keeps you away from home. In this case you may decide to change jobs to get these benefits.

As with any change, be cautious. You don't want to add to your stresses by changing job too soon (assuming you can get one), and it is always a bit unpredictable whether or not a new job will really work out: the actual terms and conditions may not be as described at the interview; uncongenial workmates can make a potentially good job a disaster.

Beware, too, of downgrading the job you do in the hope of having less stress. You may feel your loss of status more keenly than you imagine, and in this way add to the stresses of life. Also, making do with less money is something that needs careful planning.

Getting a job

If you have not been in paid employment, you face an even greater challenge. It may well be very hard to break into the jobs market, so seek advice as to how to go about it.

It may be easier to decide what to do if you have previously worked, especially if you have skills that you could polish up readily. Were you, perhaps, a secretary, a shop assistant, a schoolteacher, a computer programmer? Whatever you did for a living, even if you haven't kept your hand in, it should be possible to take it up again. There is probably an evening class you could attend for a short session until you are competent once more, or you could take advantage of the various training schemes on offer.

Often the institutions that offer training courses also provide guidance on how to go about getting a job: the right way to apply, how to handle the interview, and so on. A good written application, properly presented, can go a long way to helping you get a job.

Nevertheless, you may have to be prepared to begin with one or two temporary jobs. They provide valuable experience and proof to other employers that you are a good candidate for a permanent job.

Unless the decision needs to be immediate, this can be the time to reassess your personality, which may have become submerged in your daily routine. Many Christians agree that committing the entire situation to God and trying to wait patiently for clear indications of what to do leads towards calmness of mind.

Into business

Setting up your own business can be an option. If you offer a service, you can build up a workload without any great investment. For example, if you can mow a lawn, clean windows, cut hair, cook, decorate or sew, you could be in great demand. An easy way to get your name known is to do your first piece of work for a friend or someone you know in the neighbourhood. If it goes well and complimentary comments are made, not only will your confidence be increased, the orders will soon start coming in.

'If you have a car it may now prove too expensive to run and maintain, but a car spells freedom and independence. If you work out the cost of fares on public transport for your family, the cost difference may not turn out to be so great. Make enquiries locally and find out if a shop or a firm would employ you as a driver, perhaps part-time. Would it be possible to run a private taxi or mini cab service? To do this you will, of course, have to fulfil all the legal requirements and be comprehensively covered by your insurance company.

You business may begin as a lucrative hobby, but if you decide really to set up in business you must get it properly organized. You should talk to the following:

○ your bank manager

○ a solicitor

○ an accountant

If you plan to run a small business from your home, you will have to consult the local byelaws as you may need planning permission. If you are in rented accommodation, you will also need the consent of the landlord.

Other organizations are willing to give free advice to small businesses: it is worth finding out which ones are to be found in your area.

Earning at home

For people with commitments in the home, such as the care of small children of dependent relatives, this can be the ideal way of supplementing the family income. It allows flexibility and does not entail the expenses involved in travelling, dressing well, buying food out, and so on.

Be cautious, however, in what you undertake. Sadly, some advertised schemes are confidence tricks. If you are asked for money before you can join a home-working scheme, beware: the offer may not be genuine. Even honest schemes can be disappointing: surveys have shown that many home-workers earn a pittance, not enough to make it worthwhile. Before you decide what you would like to do from home, make extensive enquiries in your area.

12
Different Types of Bereavement

DEATH OF A PARENT

Many families these days are fragmented and scattered rather than the close-knit units of a century ago. The degree of involvement with parents is very often less than it used to be, and the loss of a mother or father in adult life is usually accepted, at least on the surface. Our lifestyle, for example, may not change too much on a day-to-day basis.

Nevertheless, when a parent dies, we often experience feelings of guilt and remorse. We reproach ourselves for not appreciating them more when they were alive, for not visiting them more often, for not doing more to help them. We remember our unkindness or impatience.

If a relative has grown difficult with age and was living with us in a small house, we may remember the times we half-wished they'd die or that someone else would look after them. Now that this wish has been granted, we may torment ourselves with regret. We wish we could call them back and say, 'I didn't mean it.'

Many children, going back to the room or house where a parent has passed the final years of life, realize with shame what a difference another coat of paint would have made and how little time it would have taken to do. On going through their parents' belongings, they realize too late how much small things like letters and postcards and snapshots had meant to their mother or father and how infrequently they had been sent. The death of a parent always shocks us, even when it can be seen as a 'merciful release'. A basic security has been taken away, a lifeline cut.

Not all feelings, of course, are of regret. In cases where there has been a close relationship, the feelings of loss, pain and intense isolation can be as debilitating as with a partner. This is often most acutely felt after the death of a mother because then the most fundamental link and most basic relationship of all has been severed. Some adult children who had enjoyed a close relationship with their mother have described 'an ache inside', allied to the cutting of the umbilical cord.

However physically or emotionally remote the relationship had become, there is a sense that there is no one to run back to. C.S. Lewis wrote that the task of dismantling what had been the family home, with all its childhood memories, was one of the most poignant tasks he had ever been called upon to do and affected him as deeply as the actual death of his father.

One step removed is the desolation felt by a child for a deeply-loved grandparent, which calls for sensitive comforting.

In proportion

It is important to realize that such regrets are natural and that the dead parent may well have felt impatience, annoyance and exasperation with *us*. Family life includes conflict as well as love. We have to accept remorse as part of our mourning, not glossing over past attitudes but not giving them greater significance than they deserve.

There will have been faults on both sides, and in earlier days, under less trying circumstances, no doubt both people would have flared up, calmed down and even had a good laugh over the very things which just now strike us as unforgivable.

Forgiveness

The Christian response to distressing memories of things done and left undone is to offer up our conflicting emotions to God, our heavenly Father. He knows our temperaments and family characteristics and what the pressures were. We can thank him for our parents and all they did for us; we can remember the good times and ask forgiveness for the bad, reminding ourselves that the love which enables us to make allowances for our own children is a reflection of his love which understands and forgives us.

While people are still alive, there is always time to put things right: death is final and robs us of that opportunity. But if, when they are no longer with us, we think only with love of the person we have neglected or misunderstood, and if we can learn from our experience to do everything we can for those who are still with us, then gradually these feelings of guilt will lessen and we shall be comforted.

DEATH OF A CHILD

This is one of the most bitter forms of bereavement. A real part of ourselves has been torn from us. It has been called the most dis-tressing and long-lasting of all griefs. It seems all wrong, unnatural and, for the child, completely undeserved. Death has come, not in old age, but in childhood or in the prime of life. More than in some other forms of bereavement the whole family will feel a shaking of the foundations of life itself.

The parents will experience many conflicting emotions, especially guilt. If the child died after a rare illness, there may be guilt at having passed on a defective gene. If death was the result of an accident, there may be guilt at having sent the child on an errand or at failing to see a danger. After the death of an older child, the parent may mourn the loss of a budding friendship and companionship just as they had become used to the child as a person rather than a baby. The loss of an only child will inevitably result in a more concentrated pining grief.

Genuine love

Whatever the circumstances surrounding the child's death, the parents will be overcome by remorse, rage and guilt but, again, we need to remind ourselves that impatience, cross words, misunderstandings are all part of family life. Children know when genuine love exists. They recognize when it is love that has prompted what to them may seem harsh or unjust behaviour on the part of parents.

Children see things in black and white and do not hold grudges. They thrive better on clashes where love is, than on indifference or total freedom to do as they like without love. One little girl arrived at school, sobbing bitterly. When the teacher asked her what was wrong, she said, 'Mummy doesn't love me—she never says, "Mind the road!"'

A valuable life

Although Christian parents will be as shattered by their child's death as anyone else, it is, I hope, a little easier to accept because a belief in a future life gives a proportion and perspective to this one. We are all locked up in our ideas of time, but for God time is unimportant. This means that a short and, to our minds, tragically incomplete life is just as valid and valuable to him as one of seventy or eighty years.

On loan

We all want what is best for those we love, but what we think is best for them may not always be in their long-term interest. If we believe that children are on loan from God, it becomes easier to understand that he loves them far more than we ever could, and will never let them slip from him. As events sometimes turn out, it may even become possible to be thankful that they were not called upon to face some disease or disaster which may have demanded more from them than they would have been able to give. I remember hearing one brave mother say, 'People keep saying, "She was so young—all the things she's missed"; but I keep thinking, "Perhaps it was the right time—all the things she may have been saved from."'

There is no glib or easy answer to the 'Why?' of the death of a child. Our reassurance must lie in the conviction that Jesus, who said 'Let the children come to me', will hold them in life and death and keep them safe.

Safe for ever

In an imperfect world it is no surprise to discover that only God is perfect. Even children are spoiled by the wrongness of the world. They are weak, like everyone else, and as they grow older and more able to form their own opinions, they too have to establish their own values. The most important of these, I believe, is to learn where God comes into our lives, and to love him. If we do love him, then to be with him, safe for ever, is the best thing we could ever wish for ourselves or our children. This is what Christians know as heaven. You have lost a beloved child, something you cannot understand; but what you can know, without a shadow of doubt, is that every child is especially dear to God. Because he is Love, he will hold them safe in a love beyond our understanding.

Brothers and sisters

If there are other children in the family, the parents must look beyond their own grief. Brothers and sisters will need comfort, patience and more love than ever. They must not be excluded from the emotions that will hit them just as hard, though in different ways. They must be allowed to grieve with their parents within the security of the family circle. Parents must be alive to their fear: 'Will it be me, next?' The children who are left may feel that the parents' grief indicates that the dead child was loved more than they are, so this can be an opportunity to explain that love is not limited—there is always more than enough to go round and every member of the family is valued and loved for themselves alone.

It is important that the neighbourhood, shocked by bereavement, does not add to the children's burden by conveying a sense of isolation. This can lead to an unconscious shunning of the bereaved family, people feeling that they will want to be left alone, and so the children will feel more bewildered or shut out than ever.

STILLBIRTH AND MISCARRIAGE

Many people think that a stillbirth or the death of a baby a few days old does not cause the same grief as the loss of an older child. But the wounds are just as deep and painful. The parents are swung from joy to grief almost in the same breath. They may find it impossible to accept what has happened. It is therefore important, unless the baby is grossly deformed and the doctors consider it inadvisable, that they are given the opportunity to see and hold the dead baby, or at least to be told what he or she looks like—the colour of the eyes and hair, for example—rather than leaving them to imagine the worst.

Some parents want a photograph they can keep. They may want to show this to any other children in the family, or even allow them to see the baby for themselves, which could reduce feelings of fear and insecurity. The bereaved mother should not be put in a ward with women nursing their live children but taken home as soon as medically possible to be comforted by relatives or friends and any other children she may have.

When a baby is growing inside the womb, the hormones, which are the body's chemical messengers, are telling the mother's body how to prepare for the birth. When this process is interrupted by the loss of the baby, the body is confused and takes a while to settle down. During this time, you may well feel emotional and depressed. You may feel cheated out of having a baby and wonder why yours was lost.

Grief and fears

The baby should be thought of and referred to by name. This fixes his or her personal uniqueness; no future child will 'replace' him or her. Recognizing the actual existence of the baby will help target the parents' grief.

Many mothers of stillborn children say that they have never got over the experience. Times come when they relive the disappointment and wonder what the child would now be like, had he or she lived.

The father usually has to go back to work after a few days, leaving the mother at home, still weak and emotional. This is when support from neighbours and friends is most necessary. Losing a baby is a lonely experience. Usually, the mother's most pressing need will be to talk about what has happened. She may need to voice fears about her next baby being stillborn; to express her feelings of guilt; that the doctors had let her down; even that, without a child to nurse, her health may suffer. The greatest help will be to lend a sympathetic but practical ear.

What about the father of a stillborn child? His grief will be just as great and his frustrations perhaps greater. He has the knife-twisting duty of registering the death at the same time as the birth, and perhaps having to make arrangements which will spare the mother, such as putting away the baby clothes and the pram.

Funeral

After any bereavement, the funeral is very important, even in the case of a very young child. Simply to take away the baby hinders rather than helps the parents to adjust to its death. Some parents are not even told what has happened to their baby. This can prolong their agony.

In England and Wales, any baby alive at birth or stillborn after the twenty-fourth week of pregnancy is legally entitled to a birth certificate and subsequently a funeral. In Scotland parents need to apply to the Scottish Home and Health Department in order to obtain the appropriate documents.

In all cases, the disappointment and poignancy surrounding such a sad event make it more than ever necessary for the parents to mourn their loss openly and formally, sometimes within the hospital with the chaplain or a local minister, or in a later small funeral ceremony. As after any bereavement, those who mourn need to say a proper goodbye in order to let the loved person go. The tears may be bitter but they will also heal.

Abortion

If you decided to have an abortion, you may have the added burden of feeling responsible for what you have done. This may be offset by the relief of not having an unwanted or a handicapped child, but at such a time feelings are inevitably mixed. When you have lost a child in this way you may find yourself worrying about its spiritual future. Yet Christians believe that God can bring healing and hope to every situation.

DEATH OF A PARTNER

Every couple has to face the fact that sooner or later one of them will die. It is estimated that one woman in five will be a widow before she is sixty. For most people, these facts are too disturbing to contemplate, and so, when the inevitable happens, the shock is all the greater.

It is a fact that husband and wife become bound to each other in far more subtle ways than being mere parties to a contract. When your partner dies, life loses its centre so that you feel disorientated, off-balance, wounded.

In *A Grief Observed*, C.S. Lewis wrote, 'No one ever told me that grief felt so like fear.' What will happen? we ask ourselves. What shall we do? Who will care? And, unlike other types of bereavement, this is the one we have to face alone. Only those who have been through the same experience can be expected to understand. For this reason, another widow or widower is probably the best person to turn to for help.

In the case of homosexuals who have lived most of their lives together in a stable relationship, the effects of the death of a partner will in many ways be the same as for a widow or widower. It may be even more poignant and lonely because there may not be the same degree of social support.

WHEN A FRIEND DIES

It is often assumed that the 'worst' form of bereavement is the death of a partner, but every bereavement is shattering in its own way.

The death of a friend brings a different but equally piercing sense of loss, especially for those who may have shared their lives for many years. We tend to underestimate a person's grief for a dead friend. Even when old and close friends have been physically separated for many years, there is sorrow for the loss of early shared experiences and all the ties which uniquely bound them together. One of the saddest aspects of growing old is that death gradually takes our friends from us. An old lady I used to visit explained her lowness of spirit when she said, 'Now there's no one left of my generation who remembers what things were like when we were young.'

Many people today have relationships which do not fit into the 'official' family structure. Sometimes, when a relationship is not conventional, social attitudes may make it difficult for those involved to grieve the loss of someone they deeply loved, or to discuss their feelings openly.

WHEN DEATH ITSELF SEEMS UNFAIR

Bereavement is a shattering blow whenever it strikes. Christians believe that death was not part of God's plan for the world, and certainly it still strikes many people as somehow wrong. It is easier to accept if it comes peacefully after long and happy years. If the cause of death seems particularly unfair, grief can be even more intense.

Violent death

None of us can escape the constant accounts of sudden and violent death. We are shaken; we feel outraged; we have an increasing sense of helplessness in the face of evil, especially when the victim is a child, a defenceless old person or a bystander.

Most people will know, or know of, someone who died as a result of one of the wars over the last fifty years. All too often the news bulletins announce yet another murder, another drunken driver road accident, another joy-ride victim. We can hardly bear to look at the suffering in other countries, bodies lying in the road, hatred in the faces of people holding guns, terror in the eyes of those caught up in areas of violence and conflict.

And for every death there will be those who mourn and

weep. The emotions common to all grief will be present, but heightened and more bitter. Some things are unanswerable—the endless questions, 'Why?'; the frustrations—'What a waste!'; the fear. The greatest need of those who have been bereaved through violence is for ready listeners who will soak up the anger and the hurt, refusing to be shocked by or critical of the violence of emotions which need to be brought out into the open and recognized.

Not many of us will have been affected by a violent death, and so it seems impertinent to make blanket observations and suggestions. But the vital imperative must surely be to forgive the unforgivable, however impossible that may seem and however long it may take. Otherwise, such lacerated scars will never heal and the survivors will themselves become victims.

Bottled-up resentment, anger, feelings of revenge, are the normal reactions to such dreadful experiences but, if unacknowledged or nursed, they will slowly erode body, mind and soul, producing physical illness and an emotional and spiritual instabiliity.

There have been many instances where a griever's whole life has been given over to finding out the truth of what happened, searching out the perpetrator, seeking some sort of retribution; and often other lives and relationships have been destroyed in that single-minded pursuit.

Justice should certainly be pursued and be seen to be done but, as is often said, 'Nothing can bring him/her back.' The only way to any peace must lie in gradual acceptance and the greatest possible measure of forgiveness. Equally, there have been many more examples of forgiveness against all the odds.

I remember the father of the girl killed in the rubble of a bomb attack in Northern Ireland. He refused to join in the screams for revenge; he refused to harbour ill-will against those who had planted the bomb. He said, 'I shall pray for them tonight and every night. God forgive them, for they know not what they do.'

He was echoing the words of Jesus on the cross. Jesus prayed for *his* persecutors, so telling us that even murderers, war-mongers and bombers are precious to God. Because God's own son can forgive even those who killed him, it becomes possible for us to forgive those who have killed someone we loved. Forgiveness may not seem to be just; it may appear to be weak; but as we accept the forgiveness of God for the violence that lies within each one of us, we shall find ourselves released from the treadmill of rage and self-destruction.

Suicide

That someone should choose to die upsets all our ideas about the value of life. It seems all wrong, and is incomprehensible. The inevitable effects of bereavement will be intensified; there will be much anger and bitterness as well as grief, especially if the person had given some indication of what they might do. All suicide threats have to be taken seriously: even those that are primarily cries for help should be treated with all the love and concern they most certainly deserve. Few of us will fully understand why someone should take such a step: it is impossible to see into a suicidal frame of mind and none of us can make a judgment or apportion blame. Suicide cannot be judged by the normal criteria. As always, it is those who remain alive who need comfort, uncritical help and, possibly, professional advice.

A proportion of the total number of suicides a year involves teenagers. In most cases, the parent will have to identify the body, which causes painful and sometimes permanent emotional scars. The suicide of a young person will fill other members of the family with anxiety and guilt and force them to examine all their relationships. Parents and siblings will be equally affected in personal ways and should be encouraged to mourn together, so that no one takes the 'blame' on to their own shoulders.

Most religions hold that no one has the right to take a life, even one's own. We can never know all the facts, pressures, problems, pains, despair of another person but we believe that they are fully known to God, who will take everything into account and disentangle all our motives and actions in the light of his merciful and unfailing love.

Many people worry about the destiny of those who have killed themselves and find it difficult to know how to pray for them, or even if their prayers will be accepted, since Christian tradition has always held that suicide is a sin. This prayer, by a Reverend Mother after one of her nuns had killed herself, is a confident appeal to the God of all mercy who understands and forgives.

'O God, righteous and compassionate, forgive the despair of her for whom we pray. Heal in her that which is broken and in your great love stand with those hurt by the violence of her end. Lord, be to her not a Judge but a Saviour. Receive her into that Kingdom wherein, by your mercy, we sinners also would have a place.'

AIDS

AIDS has come as a saddening and frightening blow to people of this generation. Raised to think that medicine could cure most infections, suddenly a new virus has proved intractably difficult to deal with.

AIDS can claim its victims in the prime of life. The survivors—a partner, a close friend—may find that they, too, are HIV positive; grief may be increased by fear for the future. Many grievers feel angry and resentful that they are the ones who are left to cope or to feel guilty. This is more likely if there had been unresolved problems or disagreements. Such feelings must be faced and expressed if they are not to fester away in the background and make the grieving longer and more destructive.

Finding someone to talk to is even more important for those who may feel isolated, unwanted and frightened by what has happened. We have to enter sensitively into their suffering, giving them the opportunity to talk through and sift their conflicting emotions. Self-esteem may be at a low ebb but it is just when we are in the depths that the love of God reaches out to us unconditionally, accepting us exactly as we are and helping us to accept ourselves. It is that love which can release us from all our nameless terrors. It will bring us comfort, courage and the confidence to face whatever the future holds.

NO EASY WAY

Never think you are alone in feeling as you do or that 'it's different for some'. True, enough money, loving friends, family support, good health, all these help; but bereavement is no respecter of persons or circumstances.

It is certainly no easier for the Christian. In some ways, it is harder, because Christians often feel, and are sometimes told, that they should be able to overcome these their doubts and fears. 'After all, you have your faith,' people say. Then you worry because you feel you are not coping as well as you should or that you are being a 'bad witness'.

But one aspect *is* different for the Christian—belief in a future life and in the never-ending love of God, both for ourselves and for those we have lost. This makes it easier for us to 'let go' of them. This 'letting go' is all-important (and appears to be more difficult when the relationship has been less than happy). Until we have released them we shall not fully recover our equilibrium; the sense of hopeless loss will remain. Such activities as making a shrine of the dead person's room, all too frequent visits to the grave, shutting out other people and other interests from our lives—all such refusals to let go stunt our growth and hold us in the unhappy present. Surely they would not have wanted that to be their final legacy for us.

If it is true that the scars of bereavement never entirely dis-appear, it is equally true that, if we do not let our dead go, the wounds beneath the scars will never heal.

Effective faith

In the early days following my husband's death, I dreaded the nights. I found then, as in other crises since, that I couldn't pray. Instead, familiar words from the Bible kept running through my mind: 'I will never leave you; I will never abandon you'; 'in quietness and in trust shall be your strength.'

I was so thankful, then, to have had a Christian upbringing—it seems to me that there can be no such thing as 'instant faith'; it has to be built up over the years slowly, until it imperceptibly becomes part of us. I've found that when life suddenly calls for the exercise of great faith, it's usually at a time when coherent thought—even prayer—is impossible. But that shouldn't worry us unduly. Christian friends and the whole church will be praying for us, carrying us along on their shoulders and opening a channel for God's love and strength to keep us steady.

The question we have to put to ourselves is not the all too frequent 'Why should this happen to me?' but 'This happens to other people—why *shouldn't* it happen to me?' Death is universal; it is part of our human condition and comes to us all. It should *never* be thought of as an individual punishment from God.

God does not exempt us from death by changing the general rule. When he became a human as Jesus Christ, even he willingly accepted death for us, in order to destroy the power of death. The Christian promise is that as death could not hold him, so it does not have the final word over us or those we love.

13
How Can Others Help?

After a death, everyone wants to help but we don't generally know how best to go about it. It isn't easy, because the people bereaved will usually not know themselves. They need time to take in what has happened. In the first state of shock and numbness, they may be unable to make even the simplest decisions.

Unless there has been a definite request for no letters, a note of sympathy can bring a warm touch of comfort. It should be brief and should not refer to any other matter. Don't worry about what to say—provided you write from the heart, you will strike the right note. This is no time to be formal. Here is an example of the sort of letter you could send:

My dear Paul,

We have just heard the sad news. I know you have your family with you, but if there is anything we can do to help, please let us know.

Words are little help at a time like this and so I won't burden you with a long letter, but simply assure you that we are thinking of you and praying that God will comfort and strengthen you all in these sad days.

With our deepest sympathy and our love,

Mary and John

Help from the family
The family is the obvious source of help, but not all families are dependable. Some people will have no family at all, and many other families are widely scattered. Within every

family there are likely to be strains and stresses; these may resurface at the time of a family death and many a funeral gathering has taken on the aura of a wary truce. Nevertheless, however seldom they meet and whatever the tensions between them, at the time of bereavement the family can be a source of great comfort and solidarity in the face of an uncertain future. As a widow said, 'I hadn't seen half of them for years but somehow it felt we were all close because we'd all lost one of ourselves.' Sometimes, when the dead person has been a very dominant character, the surviving members find that afterwards they are able to draw more closely together.

How friends can help

Friends have a vital role to play in helping the bereaved. Members of the family may be too involved. A friend can be

---

Dos and Don'ts

Do say	Don't say
◇ 'Come and be with us for a little while'	◇ 'It's God's will'
◇ 'You're doing very well'	◇ 'Be thankful you have other children'
◇ 'It's all right to be angry with God'	◇ 'I know how you feel'— unless you really do
◇ 'It must be so hard to accept'	◇ 'Time will heal'
◇ 'This must be very painful for you'	◇ 'You shouldn't question God's will'
◇ 'Tell me what you're feeling'	◇ 'Life goes on'
◇ 'What can I do, now, to help?'	◇ 'You're not the only one'
◇ 'It helps to cry'	◇ 'He/she had a good innings!'
◇ 'People really loved/respected/admired him/her'	◇ 'Cheer up—this isn't like you!'

---

just the person to confide in when members of the family may be too upset. What a bereaved person needs most, especially in the weeks immediately after the funeral, is someone who will be quietly available, looking in to check that all is well, ringing up to say, 'Hello, is there anything you want from the shops?', giving a hand with the small, mundane jobs which still have to be done. Such a helper must be prepared for anything—apathy, laughter, tears, even rudeness. The bereaved may unload their anguish and anger on you as the nearest person present; you must be ready to accept whatever they throw at you. The value of reliable, trustworthy friends lies in their willingness to listen, reassure, encourage and to mop up some of the mourner's inner turmoil. At the same time, positive observations on progress being made will do much to lift the spirits!

Try not to shower the bereaved man or woman with advice. Plans will have to be made, but not yet. Pity is not helpful—it turns the sufferer into an object, set apart and in some way inferior to 'normal' people. What is needed is the understanding compassion which stands alongside the other person, often better expressed by an arm round the shoulders or a squeeze of the hand backed up by practical help. Vague offers of 'anything I can do' may make the comforter feel better but will not greatly help the disorganized griever. Keeping a home running smoothly, cooking meals, doing the laundry are huge burdens to an exhausted person. Spontaneous and thoughtful acts of kindness will be much appreciated—a cake for tea, a bout of gardening, an offer to take the children to the park, an invitation for Sunday lunch. For six Sundays running after my husband died, a good friend had us all to lunch and then allowed me to sleep all afternoon while her husband took the children out. It was those Sundays that kept us all sane!

Visiting

Frequent short visits are more valuable than occasional long ones. They are a reminder that you are not forgotten. Visitors often find conversation difficult. This is understandable, because talking about things that must now appear trivial will seem wrong, and this rules out large areas of normal chat. As it is impossible to ignore what has happened, it is better to say right at the start how sorry you are.

There can be no 'right' thing to say—the only way is to speak openly and warmly and take your cue from the other person's reaction. The same approach is needed when speaking to the children—this is a time when they must be treated like adults, with dignity.

Long-term caring

Encourage the bereaved to pick up the threads of life as soon as possible. Try to include them in normal activities—not just when you haven't anything better to do. And not only in the first few, dreadful weeks. Go on caring, visiting and making the effort to see behind the answer 'Oh, I'm fine', when you ask them how they are. Months, even years, later there will be bad patches which can be worse than the first effects of grief—by sympathetically drawing them out you may be helping them over another low.

This is often the case when a married person was bereaved while still relatively young and has not remarried. A widow's life can become very empty when the children have left home and she has given up a job; a widower may be living out a lonely retirement coming to terms with unstructured days and desperately missing his former workmates.

George never complained; everyone thought he was contented and coping well with living alone. He shopped and cooked for himself, his garden was a picture, he was active in his church and cheerful to be with. It was when someone commented on the new picture which one day appeared on his living-room wall that it became clear how lonely he was. 'It's got people in it,' he explained. 'It's company.'

Single people, too, may have been very dependent on the relationship they have lost. People can overlook their distress, imagining, too glibly, that they are used to living alone.

It is important for friends not to be too forceful when giving their opinions; the bereaved person has little enough self-confidence and your apparently impregnable position will only injure it still more. Most people, given the chance to speak aloud about a problem, find it working itself out in their minds while they talk. Gentle encouragement and the suggestion of some side of it which may not have occurred to them may be all that is necessary.

Never try to force anyone to reveal their deepest feelings unless they want to—some are too personal or distressing. We have to distinguish between pity, which serves only to feed self-pity, and true comfort which strengthens. Genuine concern is what counts, plus the attempt to put yourself in their place: avoid the trite clichés which would drive you mad if they were said to you.

PROFESSIONAL HELP

As well as family, friends and neighbours, there are also those whose jobs bring them into contact with the bereaved, and who are there to give their professional help.

The church

One of the first visitors to the bereaved family is likely to be a member of the clergy. Many ministers confess that this is a side of their work in which they feel most at a loss and, like other people, embarrassed and inadequate, even when visiting a member of their own congregation. If the minister has had little experience in this area, the bereaved person may feel that he or she simply doesn't understand. They should not be disconcerted if the bereaved's faith seems shaken. It cannot be taken for granted that a person with religious beliefs will be more easily able to accept the death of someone they loved. If the death was untimely, the idea of a loving personal God may now be hard to maintain. The bereaved person may be having to ask questions for the first time.

Facile reassurance, biblical quotations and glib easy answers are all equally unhelpful in the face of such heart-searching. Nearly all the people I have spoken to say that the minister who gave them the most help was the one who accepted their grief, especially their bitter anger against God, recognized that there was nothing he could say to alter the fact that death had taken place but, at the same time, managed to convey that they were not alone in their suffering.

On the other hand, the church *has* got something to say. A woman was grieving inconsolably for her husband, tragically killed. When the vicar came, she only said, 'Go away, you can't help me.' 'I *can* help you,' he told her. 'I am here on God's behalf. I have his authority to bring you comfort and peace.'

Medical help

Today, most people turn more naturally to the medical profession for help than to the church. Seventy-five per cent of bereaved people visit their doctor during the first six months after the death. This seems to reflect the attitude that grief is an illness which can be treated, rather than an emotional process which needs to be worked through. Regrettably, only a few minutes can be allotted to each patient these days. But time is just what the bereaved person needs—no one in this position can marshal the thoughts to describe their symptoms and feelings adequately in five minutes.

A busy doctor, who may also feel helpless and ineffectual in this situation, is often forced into prescribing drugs without the advice that should go with them. Sleeping-pills are the most sought and most widely prescribed; tranquillizers and anti-depressants are given for daytime relief, as well as various tonics and vitamin preparations. Drugs have their place, but more important by far is the listening ear, reassurance, and a promise that the person can come to the surgery whenever they need to.

Doctors also have to understand why angry words may be hurled at them—this is the urge of the bereaved to rationalize death and to find a scapegoat. The bereaved person needs confidence in the doctor to understand grief and its effects. Here, the doctor can help by pointing out that sometimes life is tragic, there are some things that can't be drugged away and anything which aims only at suppressing the grief and pain is more likely to prolong the course of mourning.

Counselling support

Health visitors and social workers are available to see bereaved people and can help a great deal in providing support. They can tell a young widow it is natural that she finds the children difficult to cope with, while watching for any sign that the pressures are becoming too great. They can, above all, listen objectively, give a problem its own proportion, and give advice from their considerable experience.

Sometimes, a radio phone-in can provide a uniquely supportive role. Bereaved people who are lonely, frightened, unable to sleep, needing to talk to someone, have discovered the sympathetic, encouraging, yet neutral ear of an anonymous presenter, sometimes backed up by other sufferers going through the same experience. For many, this contact has literally been a lifeline.

Remember too that the Samaritans are available to talk to at any time. Their number will be in your phone book.

Help from organizations

Many organizations have been set up to help the bereaved. Such clubs must be seen not as ends in themselves, but as stepping-stones between one stage of life and another. Otherwise, the danger is that they will become inward-looking and their members may feed on each other's fears and depressions instead of overcoming them. The organizations themselves recommend that their members leave once they feel strong enough. But in the early months many people are relieved to discover that they are not alone and that their reactions to what has happened are widely shared. (See the list of organizations in the chapter *Preparing For Bereavement.*)

Self-respect

The aim of all those wanting to help the bereaved should be to raise their dignity, self-respect and self-dependence. If there are very young children, an offer to babysit will be appreciated as many young parents cannot afford to pay and so find themselves spending every evening at home. A vague 'Let me know if I can do something' is rarely anything more than conventional politeness. It's best to decide on something which they will need help with—the washing, cooking or shopping—and offer to do that.

If the bereaved person has to ask for help on too many levels, it will only add to the general sense of inadequacy. If you have the opportunity to help, make it sound as though you'd like to do the job—almost as though the bereaved person would be doing you a favour by allowing you to do it!

I remember having a dreadful cold and sitting looking at a basket overflowing with damp clothes when a friend dropped in, took everything in at a glance and said, 'Oh, do let me do that ironing while we talk—I can't bear washing but I love ironing and I'd really enjoy it.' She was so convincing I still don't know whether it was true or not, but I was grateful!

Occasions like school prize-givings or sports days can bring acute anguish for the lone parent, not only because of the array of husbands and wives together but because you wish the children's father or mother could see them now. The support of another person close to the family can make all the difference. The children will be pleased that they are worth coming to see and the parent will not feel so much the odd one out.

A common fear

Many people, especially women, may be frightened of going into an empty house after dark—or even in the daytime. If you have taken a friend home after a trip to the shops or an evening out, it really is a kindness to insist on going at least as far as the hall with them. There is nothing so forlorn as a silent, empty house and it is a relief to be helped over those first few minutes.

These days, especially in the city, it is likely that a woman will refuse an invitation to go out in the evening simply because she is frightened of being out alone after dark. If you suspect this to be the reason, again it would be kind and sensitive to offer to fetch her and take her home.

Epilogue

Sooner or later, each of us will have to go through the experience of bereavement. As in other areas of life, some degree of thought and preparation, rather than trusting to luck or refusing to talk about it at all, will make it easier to manage when it strikes.

Those for whom bereavement is still an unknown dread naturally fear it. They wonder how they will react, how they could possibly go on living without someone who means so much to them. They fear that nothing and no one will be able to help. Will they ever get over it?

In a sense, we never cease to grieve our losses. Out of the blue will come the darkness of 'Who cares? Why bother to keep making efforts? What does the future hold now?' But gradually we discover that the pain and the black hopelessness no longer dominate our lives. We may still be weary; the adjustments we have to make involve ongoing hard work—keeping our friendships in good repair, taking up new interests, being responsible for our own decisions—but there will also come brief flashes when we recognize in ourselves signs of new life springing from the old.

Christians believe that what gives them the necessary strength to go on living now, as well as security for the future, lies in their relationship with God through Jesus Christ. This does not mean that they are unaffected, or less affected, by the sorrows of death and bereavement, but that they have God's support and comfort to draw on when tragedy strikes, and the sure and certain hope of a life beyond death shared with God himself. This gift of new life, of friendship with himself, God offers to anyone who will accept it. It is not just for a special few.

One of Paul's letters to Christians that is in the New Testament tells us that 'perfect love casts out fear'. Love is the best antidote to fear—not our human love which can never be perfect, but God's love for each one of us, his children, according to our individual needs, perfect and complete, unfailing and never ending.

The reality of Jesus' promise, often used in the words of the funeral service, can be proved by everyone who trusts themselves to God's care: 'I am the resurrection and the life. Whoever believes in me will live, even though he dies; and whoever lives and believes in me will never die.'

J.F.R.
March 1992

Useful Addresses

Some of the main organizations in the United Kingdom that offer support to the bereaved:

Cruse 126 Sheen Road, Richmond, Surrey TW9 1UR.
  For bereavement care.

The Compassionate Friends 6 Denmark Street, Bristol BS1 5DQ.
  For bereaved parents.

BACUP 121/123 Charterhouse Street, London EC1M 6AA.
  For practical advice and emotional support for cancer patients, their families and friends.

Gay Bereavement Project Unitarian Rooms, Hoop Lane, London NW11 8BS.
  Advice and support for lesbians and gay men bereaved by death of a same-sex partner.

Samaritans The number is in the phone book.
  For someone you can talk to who will give you support in any kind of trouble.

Miscarriage Association
  Kathryn Ladley, PO Box 24, Ossett, West Yorkshire WF5 9XG.
  For parents of babies born dead before the 28th week of pregnancy.

Marie Stopes Clinic Addresses in DSS book.
  For emotional help after abortion.

Organizations in Australia supporting the bereaved are:

Compassionate Friends Inc. Bereaved Parents' Support and Information Centre, Suite 3, Rear 205 Blackburn Road, Syndale, VIC 3149.

Sudden Infant Death Syndrome (SIDS) National SIDS Council of Australia, 1227 Malvern Road, Malvern, VIC 3144.
  For those bereaved over the sudden death of a child.

National Association for Loss and Grief (NALAG)
  Branches throughout Australia. NALAG often hold seminars in coping with grief and is a very useful contact for all forms of bereavement.

Bereavement Care Centre 41 The Boulevarde, Lewisham, NSW 2049.
  Caters for all forms of bereavement. Run by Mal McKissock.

The Aids Council of NSW (ACON) PO Box 350, Darlinghurst, NSW 2010.
  Provides a counselling service for those suffering the loss of an AIDS victim.

Helpful books on bereavement from LION PUBLISHING

LIVING THROUGH GRIEF Harold Bauman	£1.35 ☐
LOSING A CHILD Elaine Storkey	£1.35 ☐
THE PATH OF PEACE Norman Warren	£0.99 ☐
WHAT HAPPENS AFTER DEATH? David Winter	£1.35 ☐
WORDS OF COMFORT	£1.99 ☐
EMMA SAYS GOODBYE Carolyn Nystrom	£4.95 ☐
KIRSTY'S KITE Carol Curtis Stilz	£5.99 ☐
GRAN'S GRAVE Wendy Green	£0.99 ☐
NO TIME TO SAY GOODBYE Paul Arnott	£3.50 ☐

All Lion paperbacks are available from your local bookshop or newsagent, or can be ordered direct from the address below. Just tick the titles you want and fill in the form.

Name (Block letters)_____

Address _____

_____

_____

Write to Lion Publishing, Cash Sales Department, PO Box 11, Falmouth, Cornwall TR10 9EN, England.

Please enclose a cheque or postal order to the value of the cover price plus:

UK INCLUDING BFPO: £1.00 for the first book, 50p for the second book and 30p for each additional book ordered to a maximum charge of £3.00.

OVERSEAS INCLUDING EIRE: £2.00 for the first book, £1.00 for the second book and 50p for each additional book.

Lion Publishing reserves the right to show on covers and charge new retail prices which may differ from those previously advertised in the text or elsewhere, and to increase postal rates in accordance with the Post Office.